The Figure in Composition

Paul G. Braun

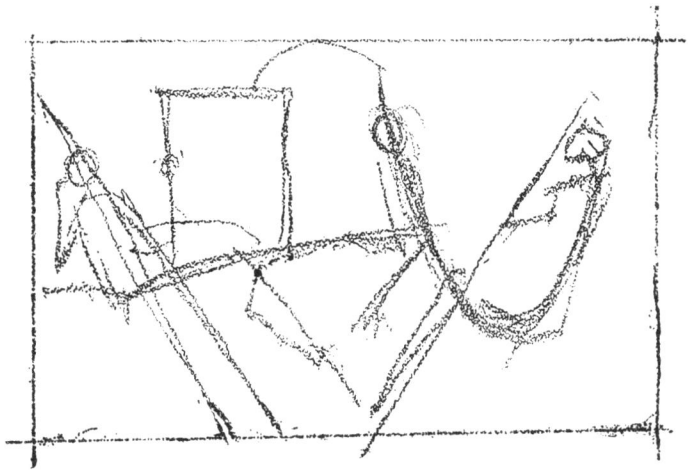

Dover Publications, Inc.
Mineola, New York

Bibliographical Note

This Dover edition, first published in 2011, is an unabridged republication of the work originally published by Bridgman Publishers, Inc., Pelham, N.Y., in 1930 under the title *Figure Composition.*

Library of Congress Cataloging-in-Publication Data

Braun, Paul G.
  [Figure composition]
  The figure in composition / Paul G. Braun. — Dover ed.
     p. cm.
  Originally published: Figure composition. Pelham, N.Y. : Bridgman Publishers, 1930.
   ISBN-13: 978-0-486-48155-5
   ISBN-10: 0-486-48155-7
    1. Human figure in art. 2. Composition (Art) I. Title.

NC765.B76 2011
743.4—dc22

2011016766

www.doverpublications.com

CONTENTS

CONTENTS

INTRODUCTION

Time and again, I have heard art directors of different periodicals declare they could spot a student's or a young illustrator's work at sight.

There seems to be something lacking.

The figures may be well drawn. In many cases, figures constructed by students are drawn much better than those of our best illustrators. The fault does not lie in their inability as draftsmen, but, one might say, in their evident desire to show the world how well they can draw the figure. In their pictures they seem to draw the figures and nothing else—and make them all of equal importance. An art director of an important monthly told me he had hundreds of figure draftsmen at his call but only a few men who realized what a composition was, and that the figure was only an important UNIT, but still a unit withal, to be kept in its place in the picture.

Well known illustrators have told me practically the same thing, that the foundation of all good pictures is found in their design—the relative value of the different units and not in the cleverness of the hand or technique.

These pages will be devoted to the study of the figure with that end in view, i.e., the figure subordinated to, and only a UNIT in the composition.

The book is designed primarily for the use of teachers and students who have some knowledge of the figure and design; to suggest pathways to be followed until the student discovers new ones for himself.

P. G. B.

ARRANGEMENT

In all compositions and illustrations the figure occupies a given space, so we will start our study by making our drawings within such space or spaces.

Make your sketches small—you won't have room for a lot of unnecessary detail. On your drawing paper place two marks about five or six inches apart. Within that space the entire figure must be drawn.

Pose your model in a simple standing or sitting position and start to draw. Carry the sketch about as far as shown on the opposite page. Stop and compare it with the model. Notice the big shapes, the torso, the hips, their movement and the length of the arms and legs in comparison with the rest of the figure. Study the sketch carefully and know what must be done to it before going ahead.

Work swiftly, but give a lot of time to comparing your model with your drawing.

After constructing figures as suggested in the preceding pages and using only the big simple forms; the next problem is to place such a figure in a given space.

Construct a simple rectangle and place in it an extremely simple memory sketch of a figure doing something, anything. Take time to make pleasing arrangement within your rectangle.

When you are satisfied with your design, pose the model in the action of the sketch and draw it simply and accurately; by that I mean, keep the big forms simple, the proportions correct and the action alive.

Spend more time comparing the sketch with the model than in drawing.

Learn to know the big shapes, how they move and their relationship in action.

Keep up this practice using all sorts of rectangles and figures in any conceivable action.

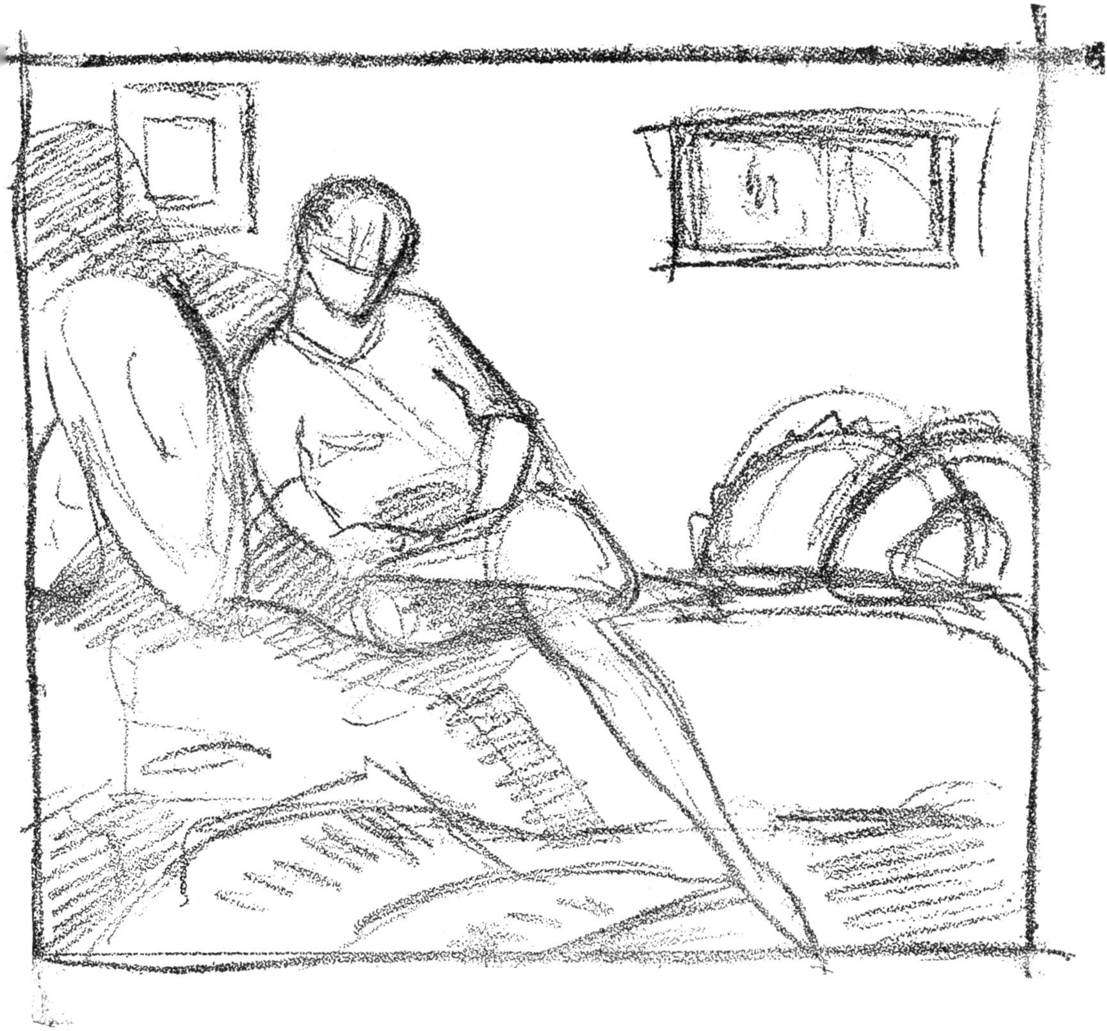

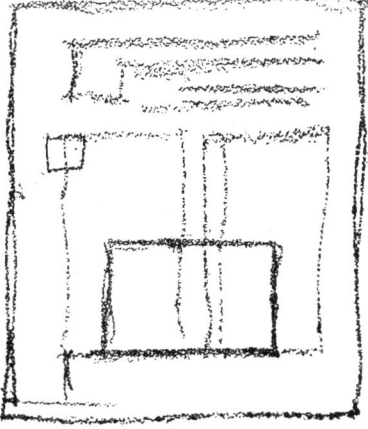

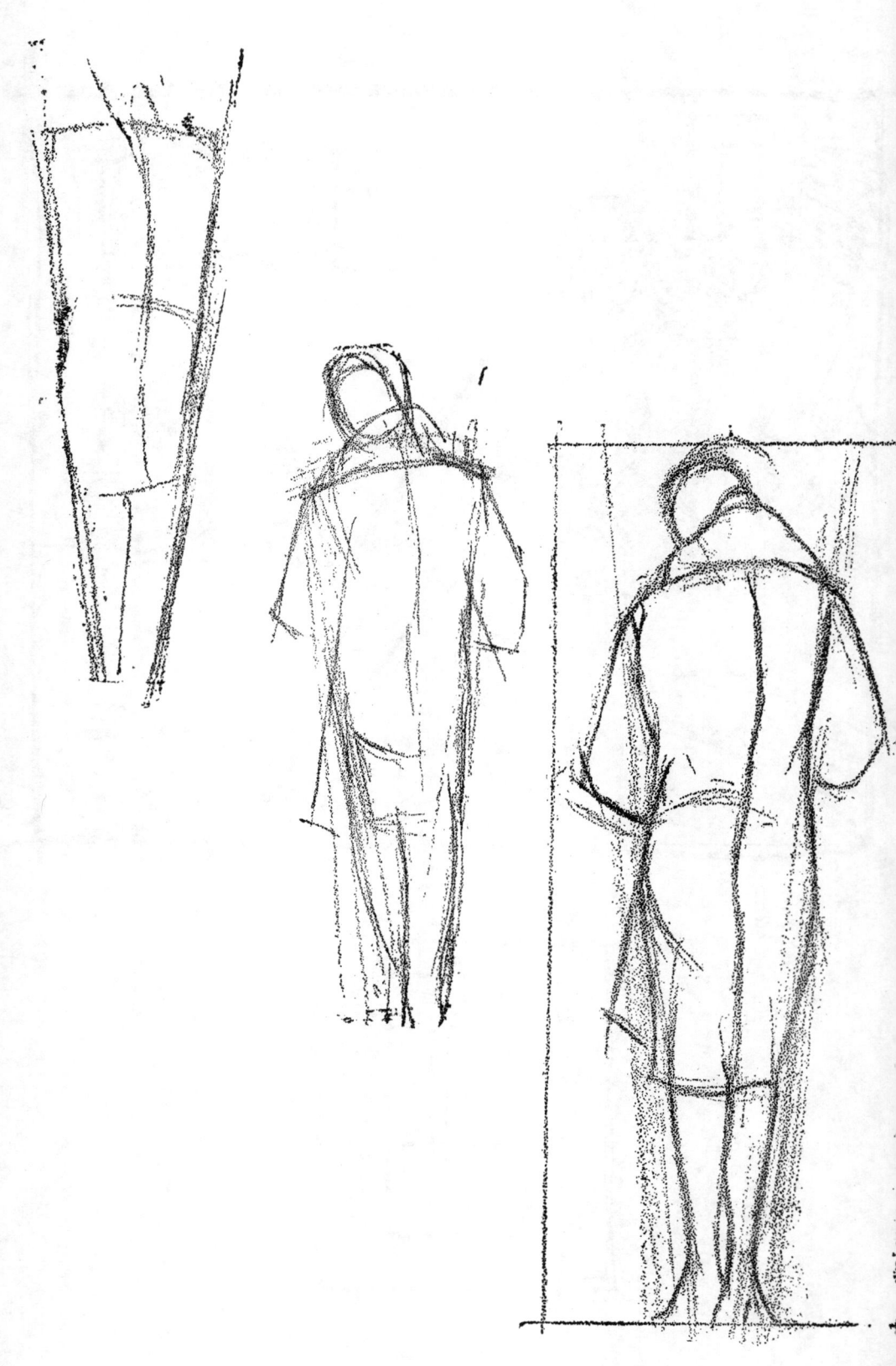

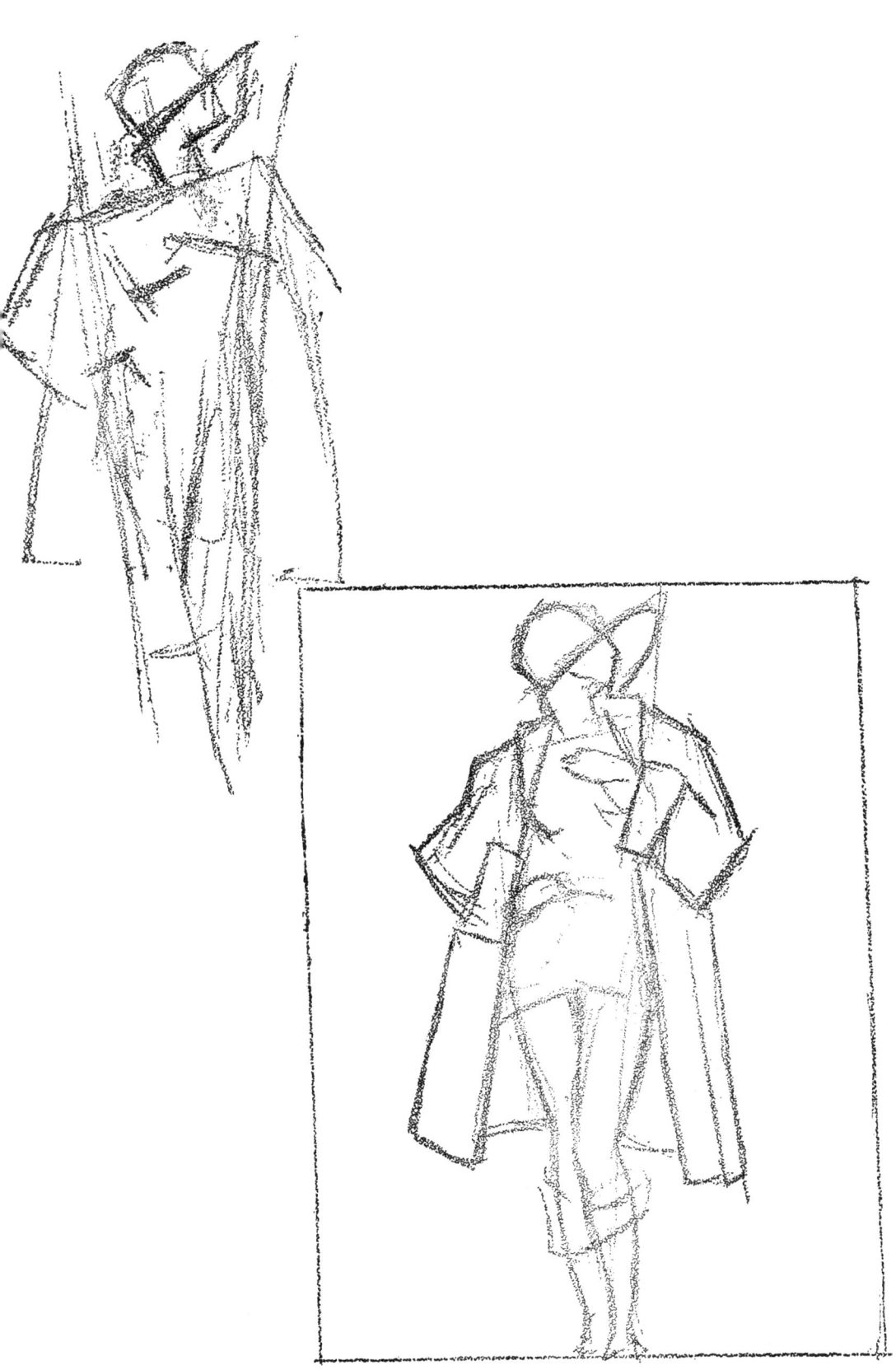

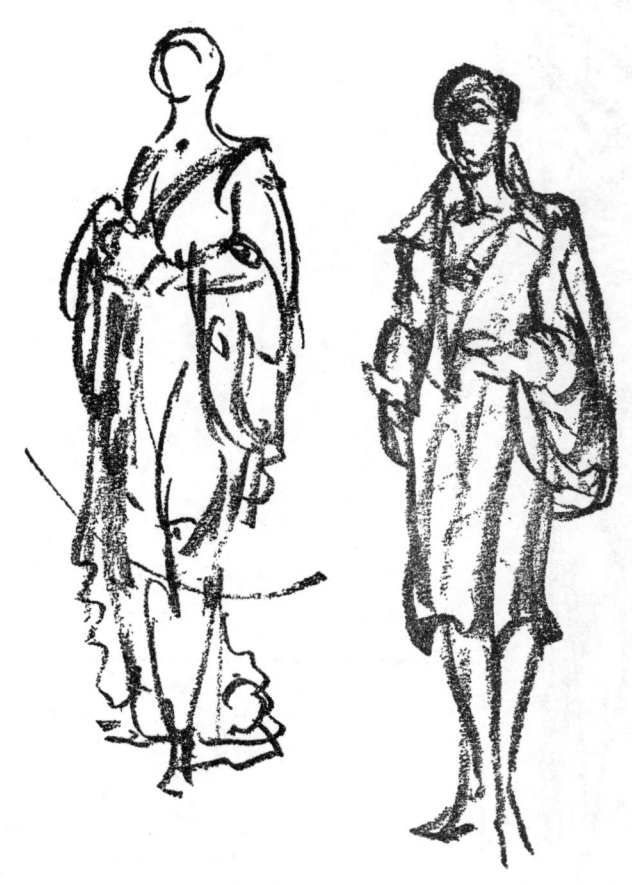

THE SINGLE FIGURE

In drawing a single figure, there must be an action movement to a figure and an inaction movement. The action side should be drawn with angular or jerky lines while the opposing or inaction side should be more rhythmic or serpentine. These lines should be made as long as possible—do not begin at the top and draw down the figure in portions. There must be no patching together of pieces—or little bits—the long lines must indicate the figure as a whole from the beginning. If this procedure is followed the proportions and balance will be seen at once to either be right or wrong.

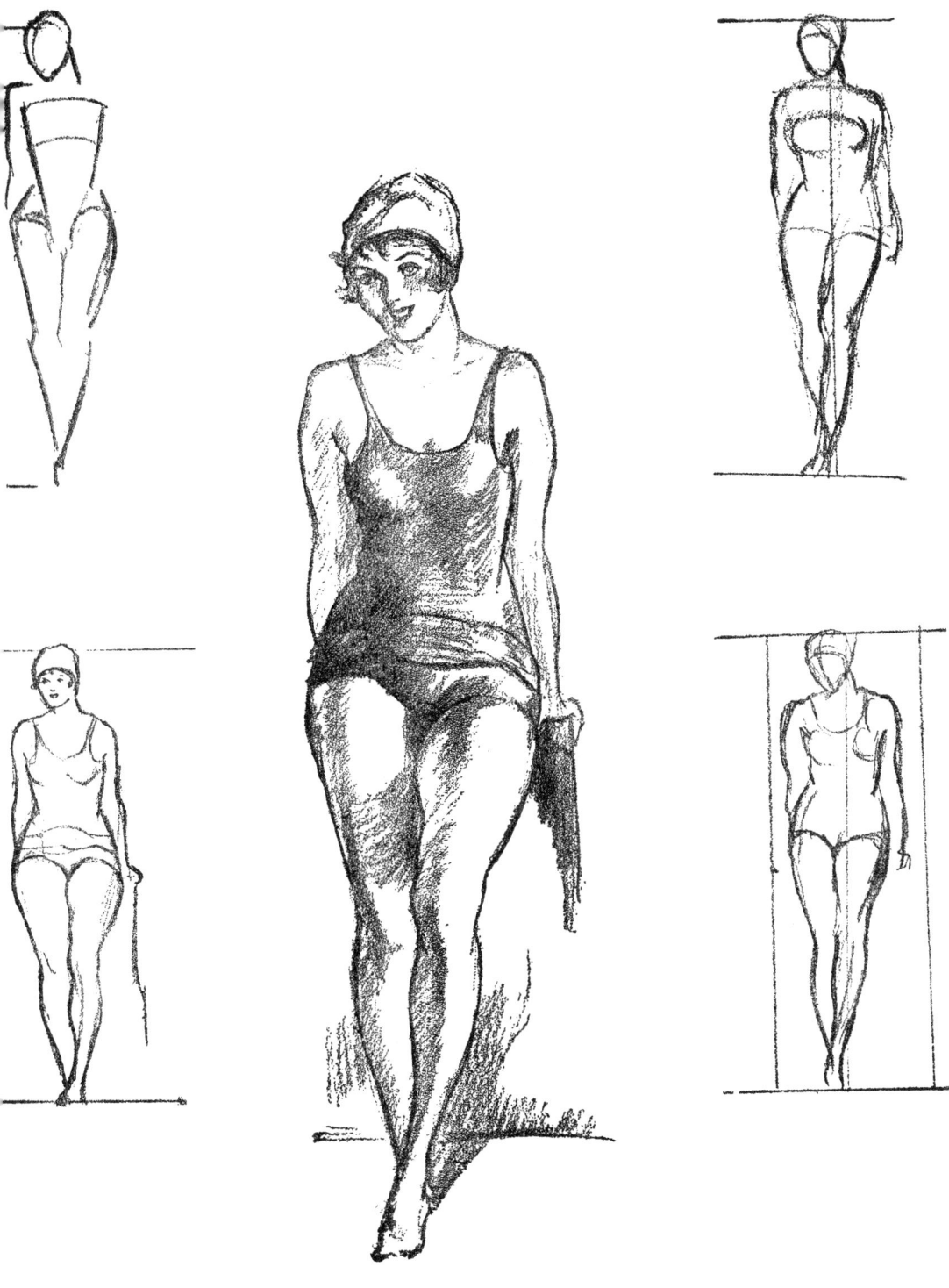

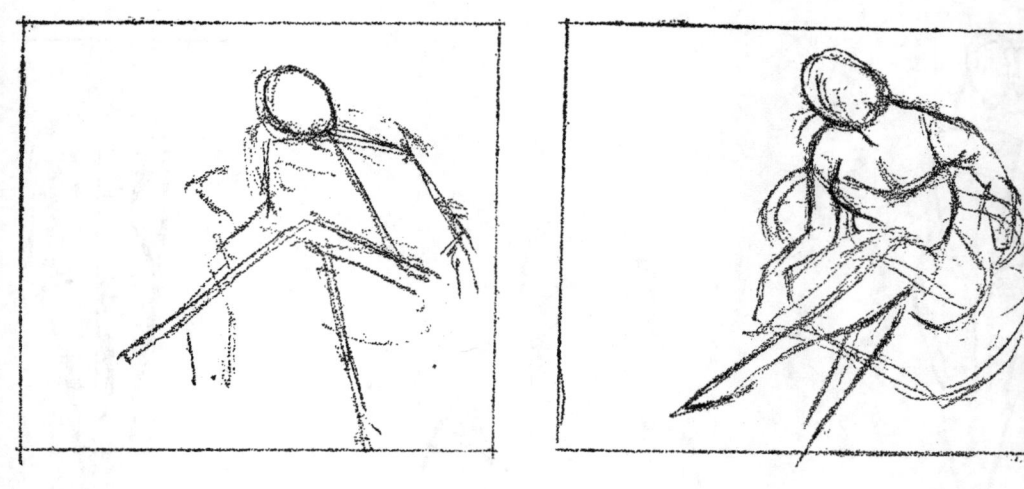

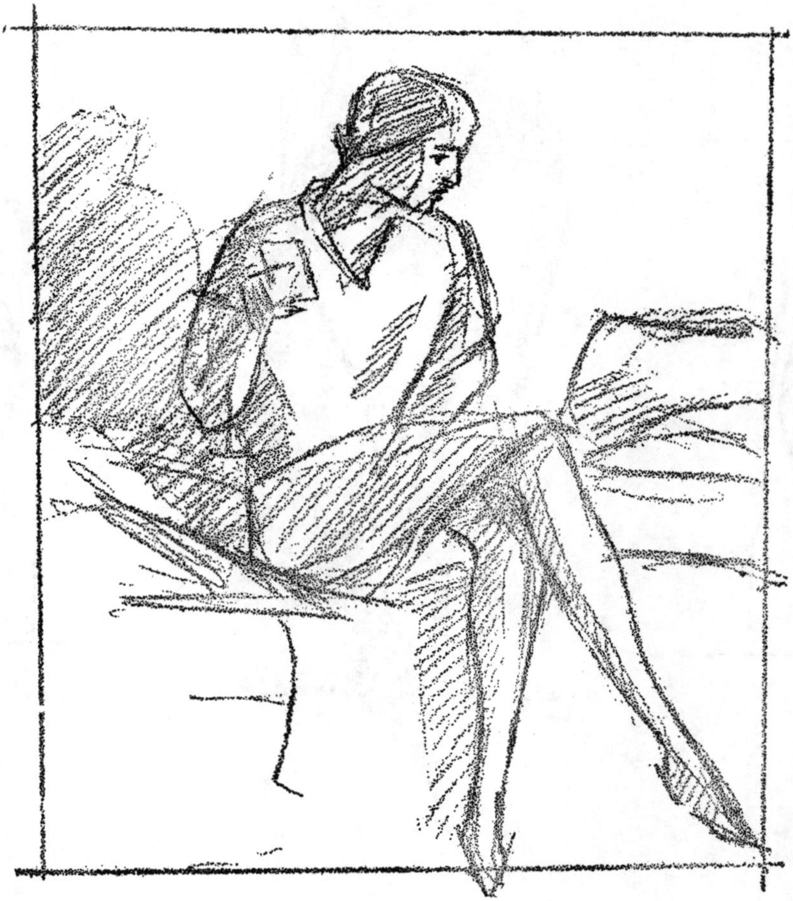

SINGLE FIGURE PROPORTION

When beginning to draw the figure great care should be given to the general proportions. The best method is to find the centres of noticeable parts, such as taking the centre between the top of the head and the foot the figure is standing on. This divides the figure into two halves. Then by measuring divide these halves again into halves or thirds. It is always easier to compare measurements that are equal than those that are not equal.

To train the eye to see these proportions correctly without having to measure try to look at the several parts of the figure, one after the other, so as to become acquainted with their appropriate relative sizes. This is the ultimate goal.

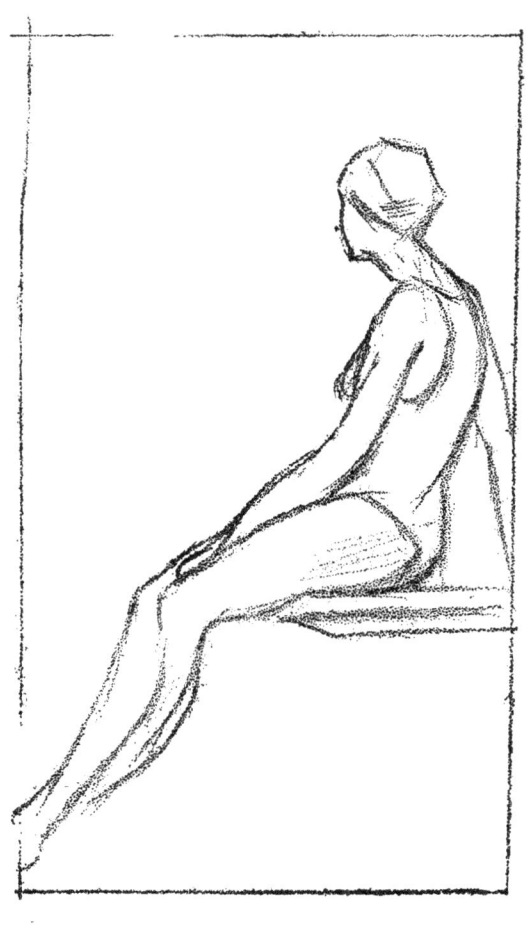

ARRANGEMENT OF A SINGLE FIGURE WITHIN A BORDER

There is another sort of harmony which is not so much a matter of leaving out things as of arranging them, and particularly applies to pictures with persons in them. Not only should the persons be necessary to our picture in the arranging of it, but they should *seem interested* in our picture. How often have you seen a picture of a group where one person is trying to make us interested in something *outside* the picture; or where a person is just about to step off the edge of the picture? Examination of pictures will show you that the rule is often obeyed with good effect and is never disobeyed without disaster.

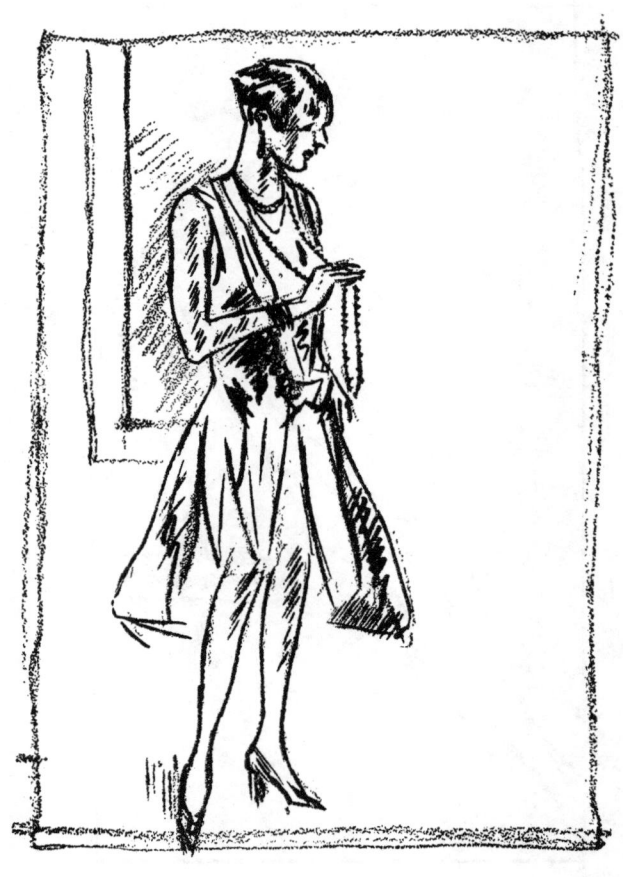

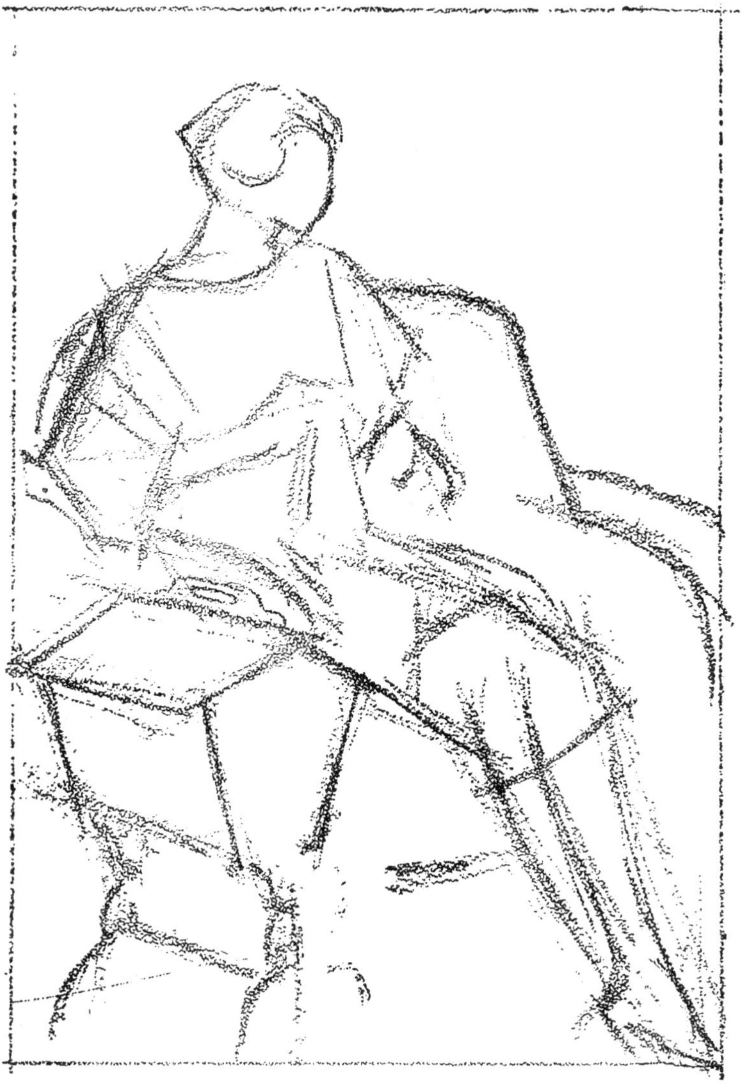

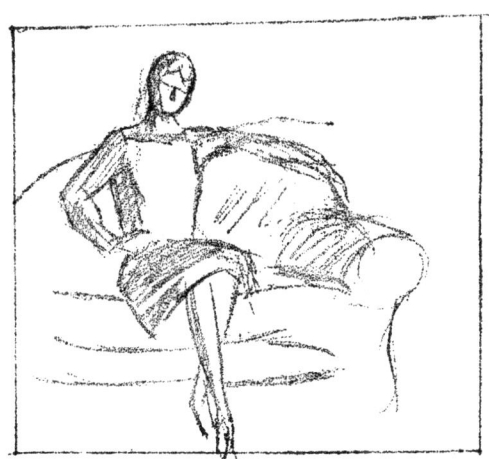

ARRANGEMENT OF TWO FIGURES WITHIN A BORDER

Construct a simple rectangle of any proportions. In it place a memory sketch of two figures doing anything—one standing, one sitting—both sitting—one explaining a proposition to another—one man and a woman, two women—anything—only tell something—something your people are doing—something human and alive. It is important to have your figures doing something natural—something anyone could recognize himself doing.

Tying the composition together plays an important part in the development of the picture. Invisible lines that run through the figures and decorations should be tied one to the other—merging and carrying through. Make a pleasing arrangement in the rectangle with straight lines, fast lines, curved lines, graceful lines, up and down the composition: look for them, use them, groups of things tied to one another by lines that carry through.

Make new compositions using these ideas. Note the improvement. Don't be satisfied until you have pumped yourself dry of suggestions. Keep the things simple throughout.

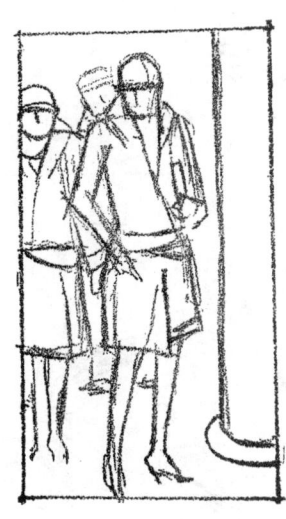

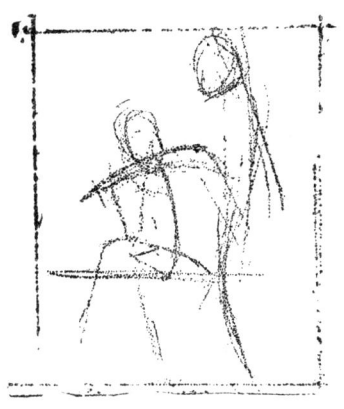
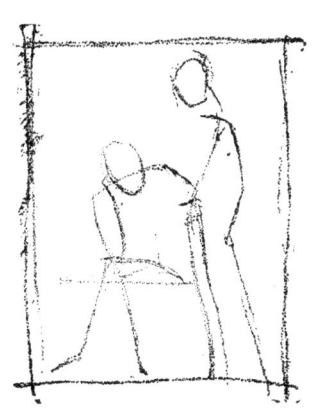
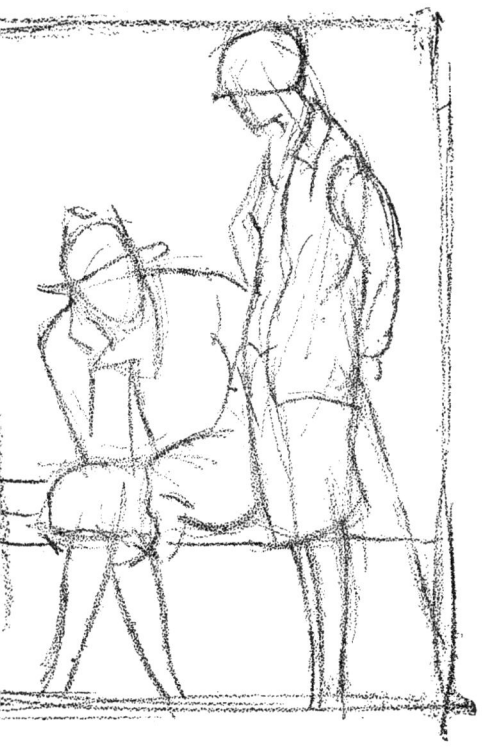
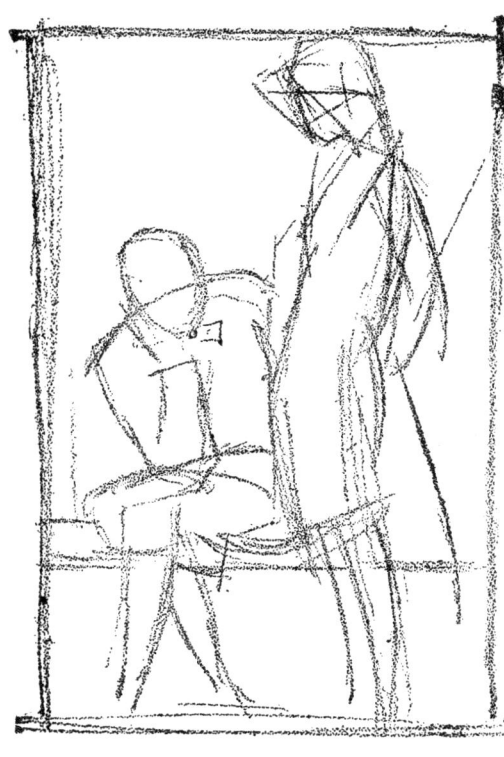

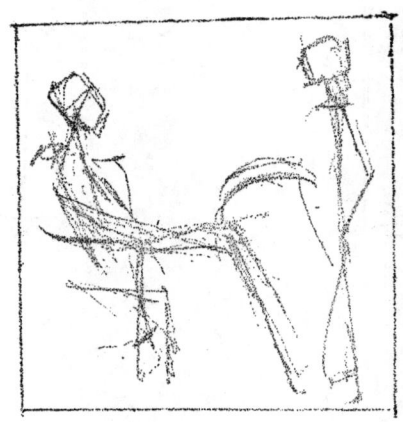

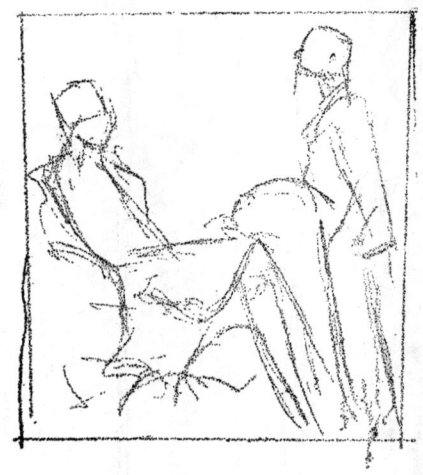

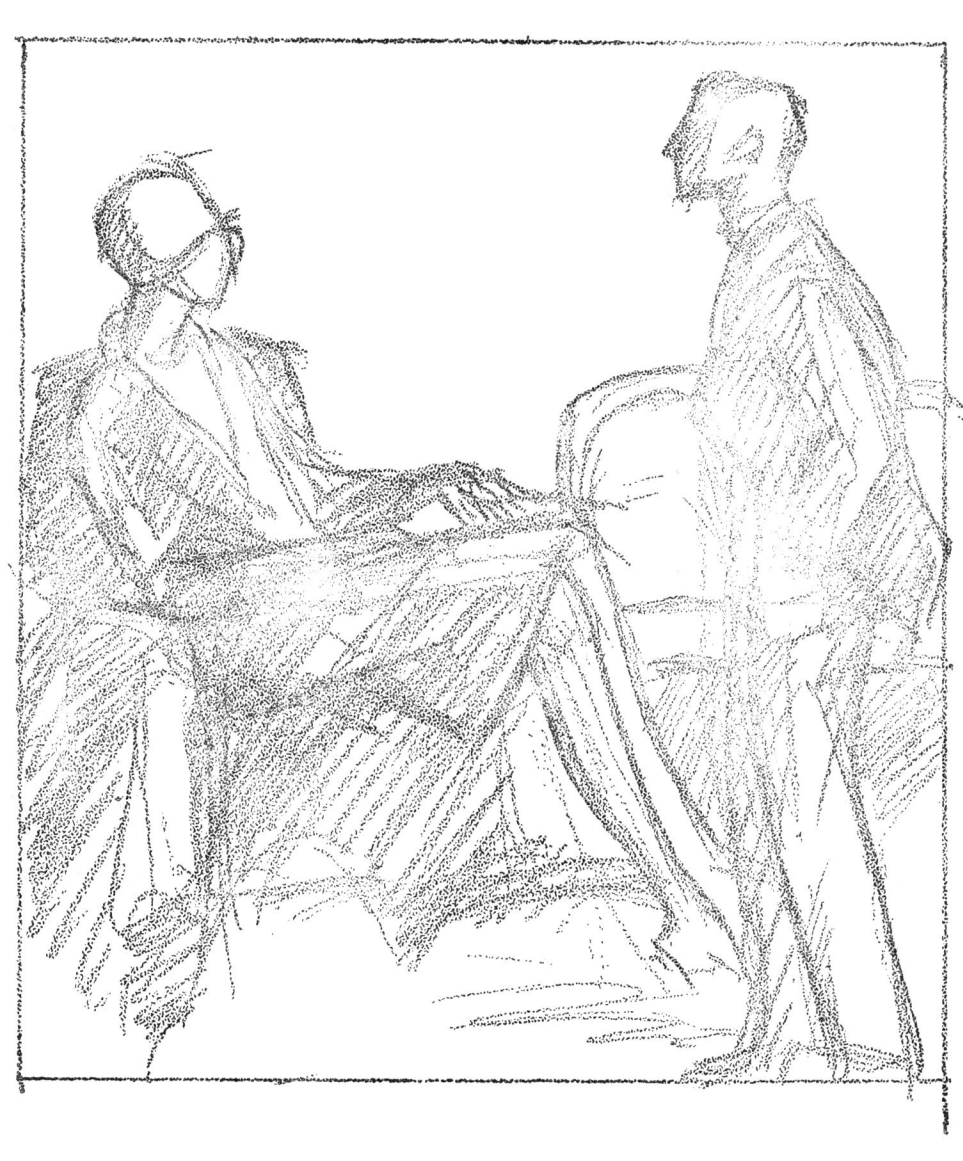

LIGHT AND SHADE

Pose your model in an interesting, easy side view position. Take your place far enough away to allow you to see the ENTIRE figure without any trouble.

Mark off the figure's space on your paper. In it place the general direction of the figure's movement and other lines denoting arms and legs. Be sure the proportions are correct. All this should be done in very LIGHT lines.

Suggest the head with an oval. Note the distance between the chest and back. Compare that distance with the width of the waist. Try to carry the swinging line of the figure through the entire sketch.

Carry your drawing through the different stages, gradually refining it.

The use of light now becomes an important factor.

If one draws a cube, it can be shown to be solid by placing a tone on one side. The light seems to be coming in a certain direction.

Darken another side and the light now comes in a different direction. The cube is still solid, so that changing the location of the shade does not interfere with the form. The same applies to your figures.

Use the shade only to show form at this stage.

Draw several simple objects from models.

Change the light in your drawings and still keep them solid.

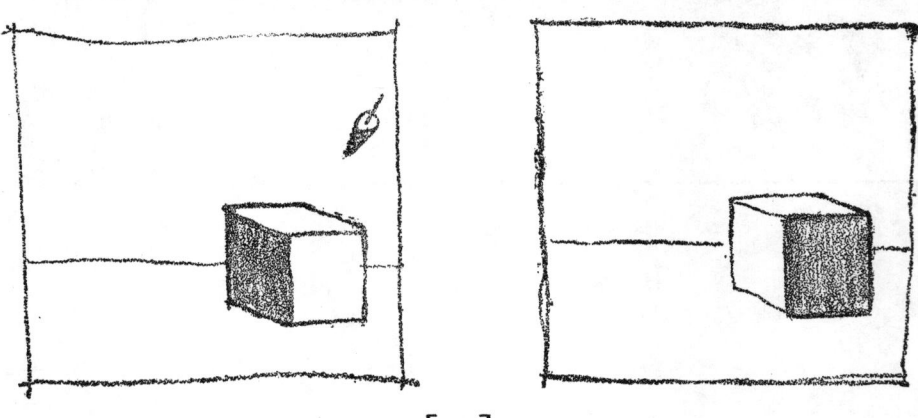

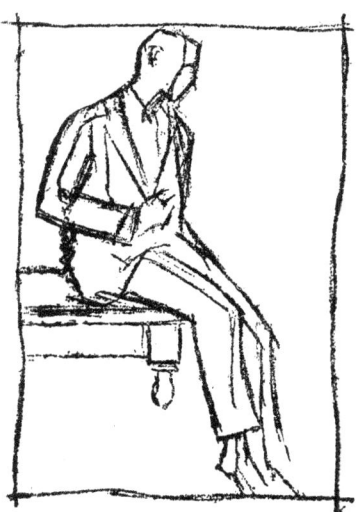
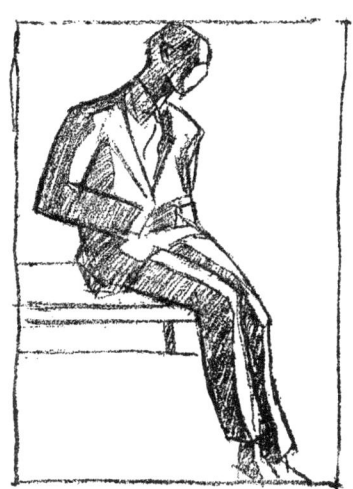
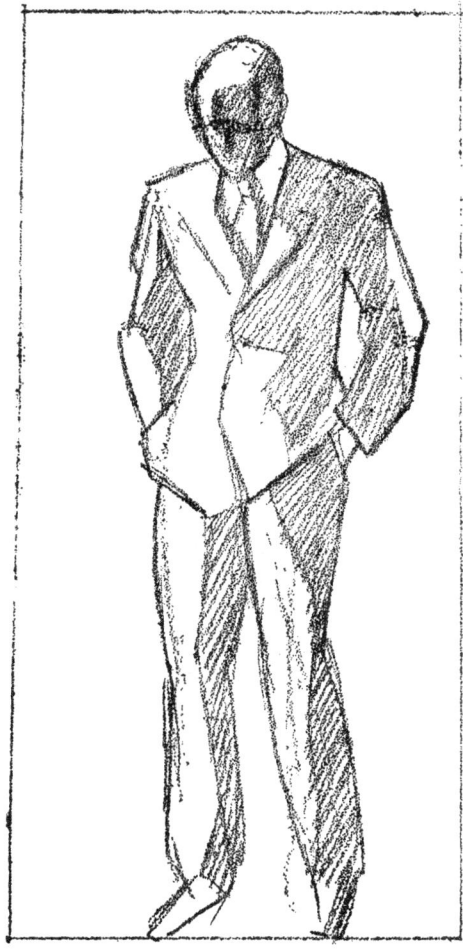

THE DRAPED FIGURE

Use a simple skeleton pattern in the making of a memory sketch. Rearrange the sketch over and over until you have something that pleases you. When you are finally satisfied with your pattern, construct a new figure similar to the one that pleases you. Pose the model in the action of the sketch. Draw both figures lightly and see that they occupy the same proportionate space. Compare them with the model, first one, then the other, alternating, never finishing any single figure.

As before, consider only the big, simple shapes—the head-shape—the torso—the legs and arms. Disregard all detail. If possible, when making these drawings completely surround them with light, so you will not be confused by the illusion of the light and shade.

Get all the proportions correct—the right relationship between the big shapes.

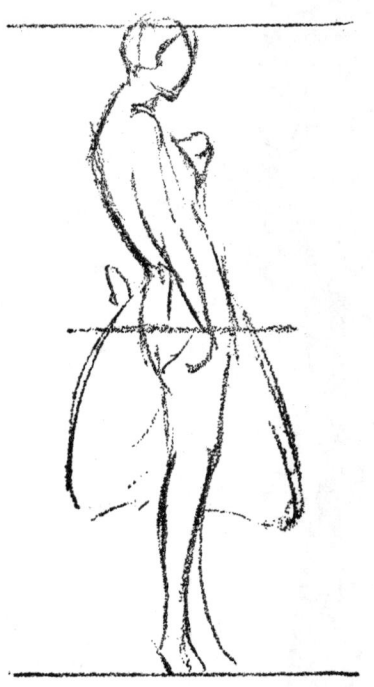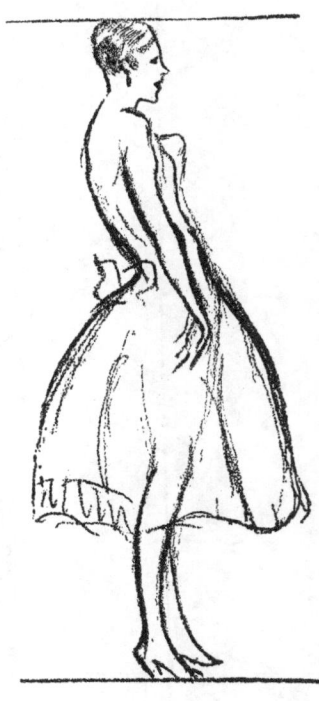

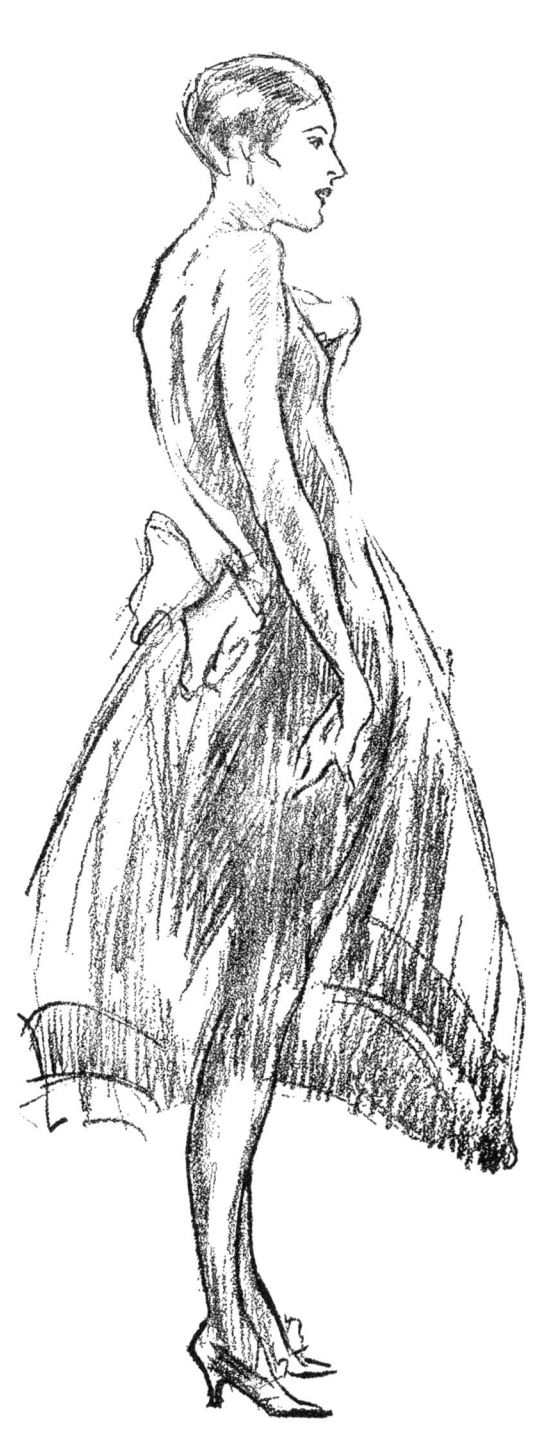

DISTRIBUTION OF LIGHT AND SHADE

The sketch on the opposite page is taken from a composition created by an illustrator of great ability. His work appears in the best magazines, yet it is the essence of simplicity.

The drawing is left unfinished to show how it is worked all over at the same time. Note the massing of form to fit an abstract dark pattern. All unnecessary detail is left out.

It gives an idea of simplicity, yet the figure is complete enough to be used in a composition.

Observe how simple wrinkles are used to show form and how much is left undone, yet no one could fail to see the figure is that of a modern young woman.

It seems to be surrounded with light. Note the way in which form is suggested by simple lines on the head and arms.

Note the light and dark pattern on the figure. Notice how strong light and dark suggest the form and also the simplicity of the head.

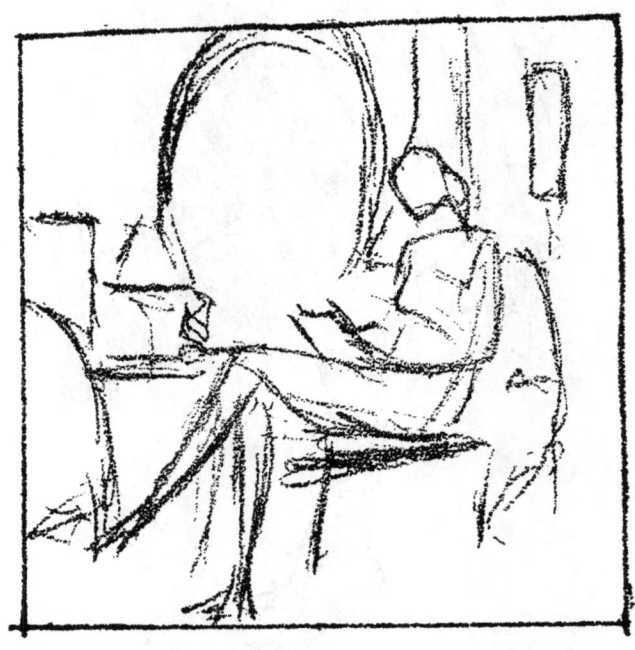

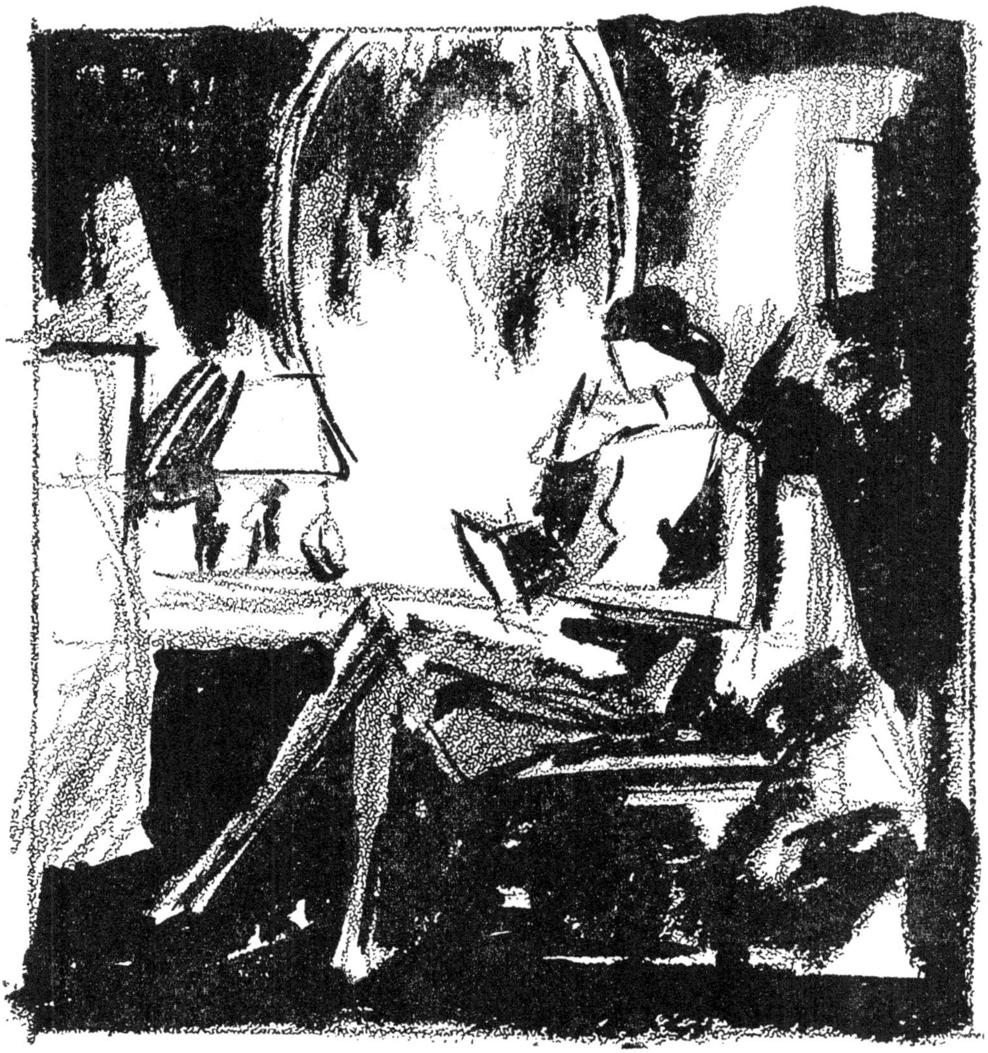

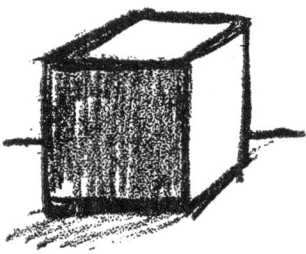

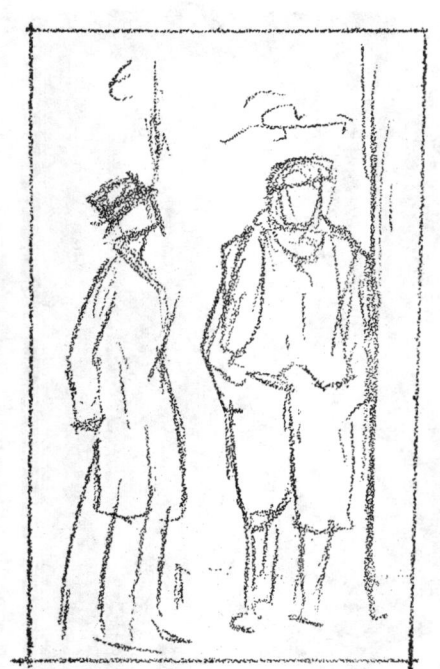 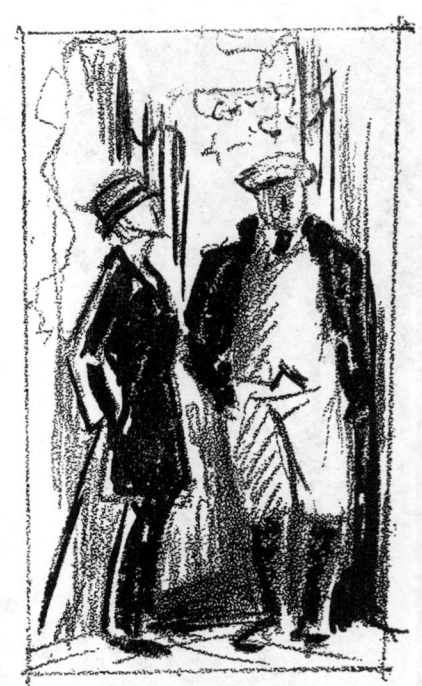

Much useless talk can be heard and many useless words read. One only learns by the practice of demonstrating to one's-self. If the student has really absorbed the ideas of simplicity in design, figure, light and dark and the relative value of features and other units in the composition, he should make pictures. These things will grow as pictures are made.

All the foregoing presupposes the student has some knowledge of design and the figure.

Abstract design should be studied and principals discovered by the student should be used in his compositions. The abstract patterns of light and shade should be applied whenever the opportunity presents itself. All compositions should be based upon such firm foundations.

Students cannot spend too much time over their plan for each picture. No matter how well drawn the figures, if the foundation is weak the picture suffers.

Study design, cannot be said too often.

Study the work of the masters, old and modern. Try to know how they arrived at their results.

[26]

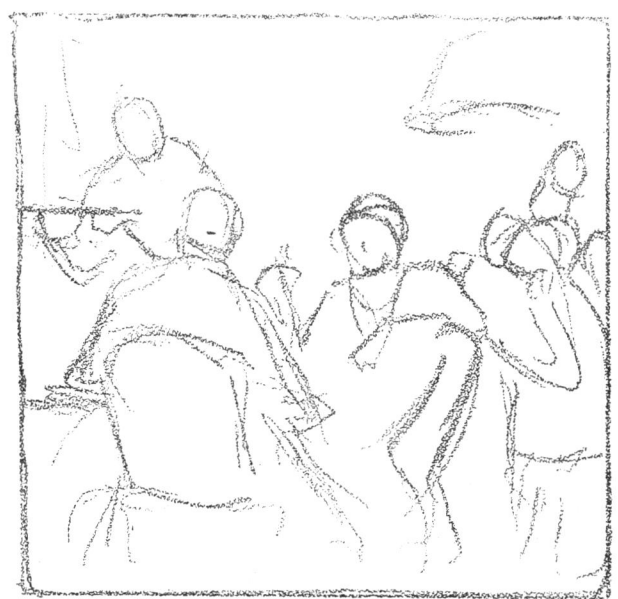

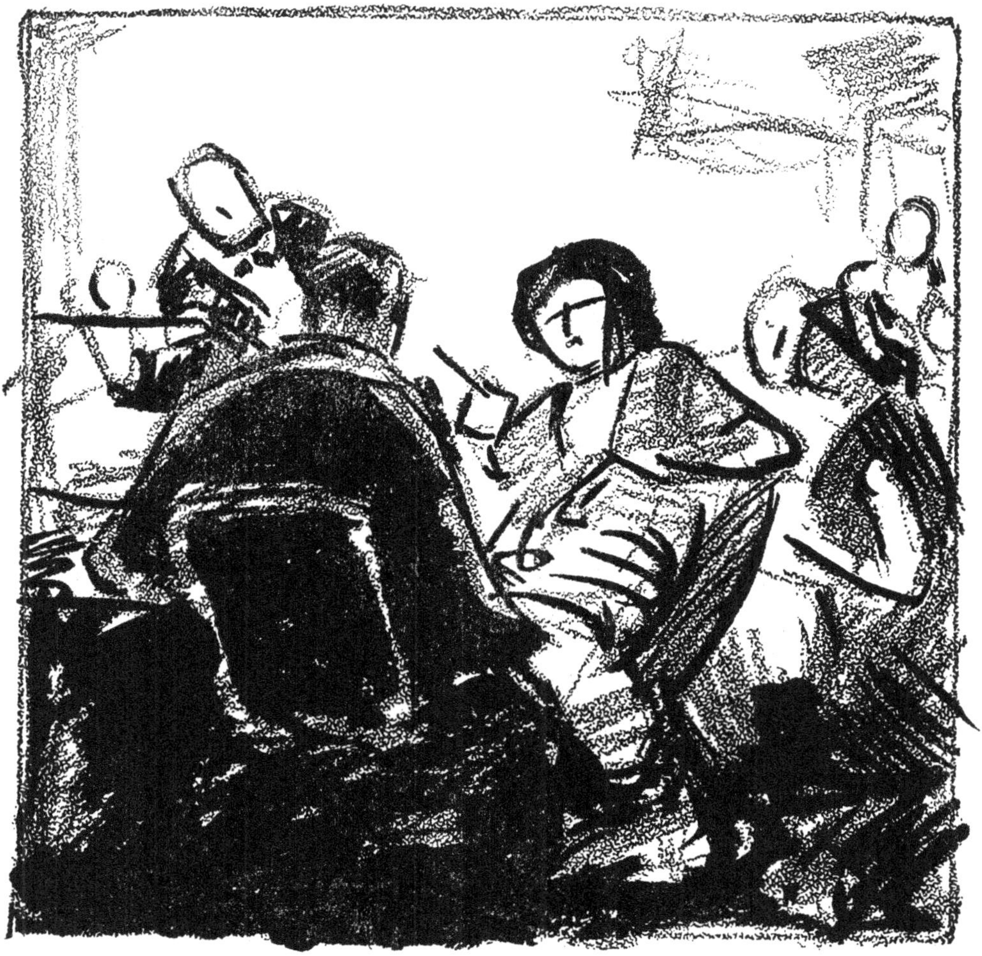

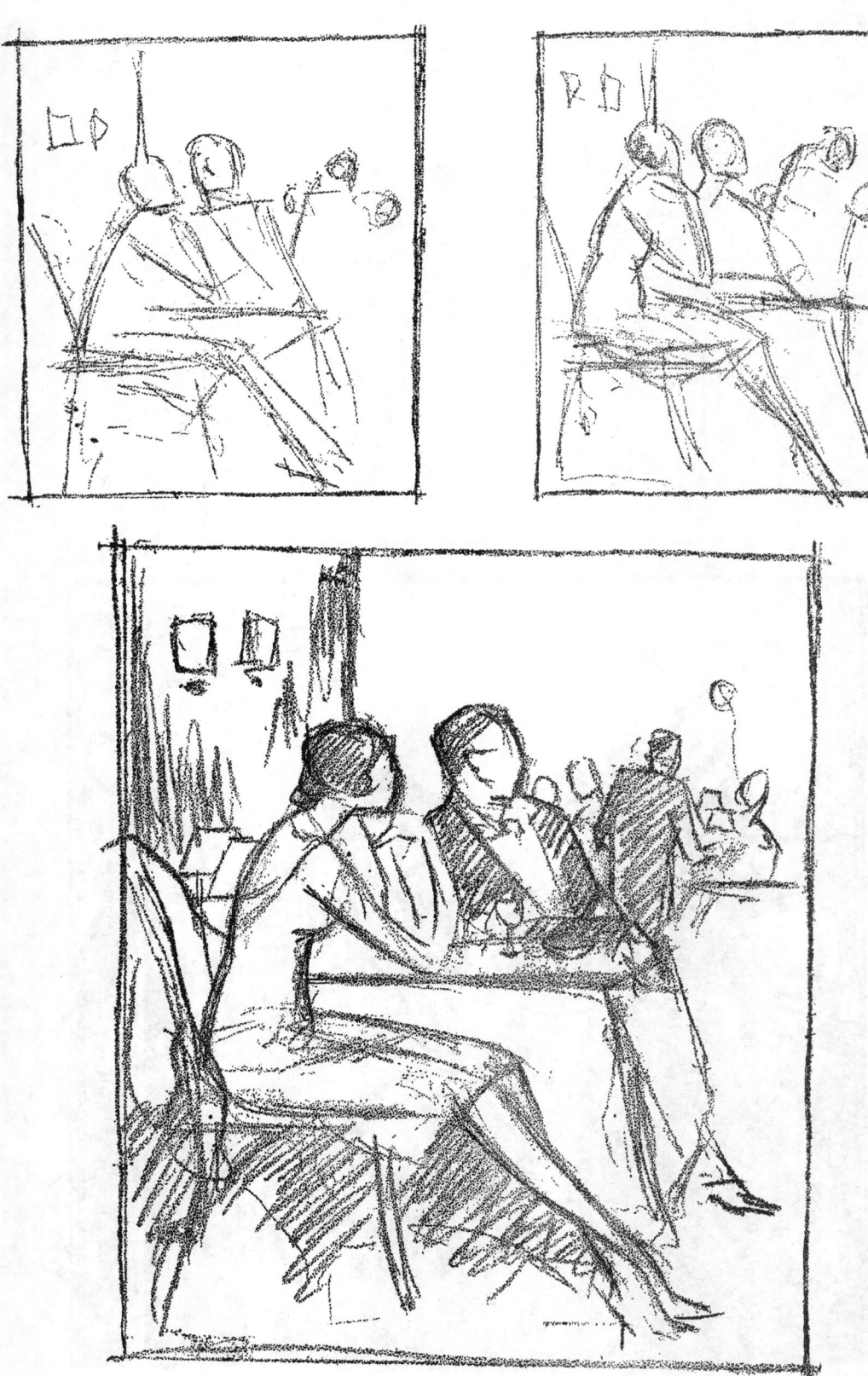

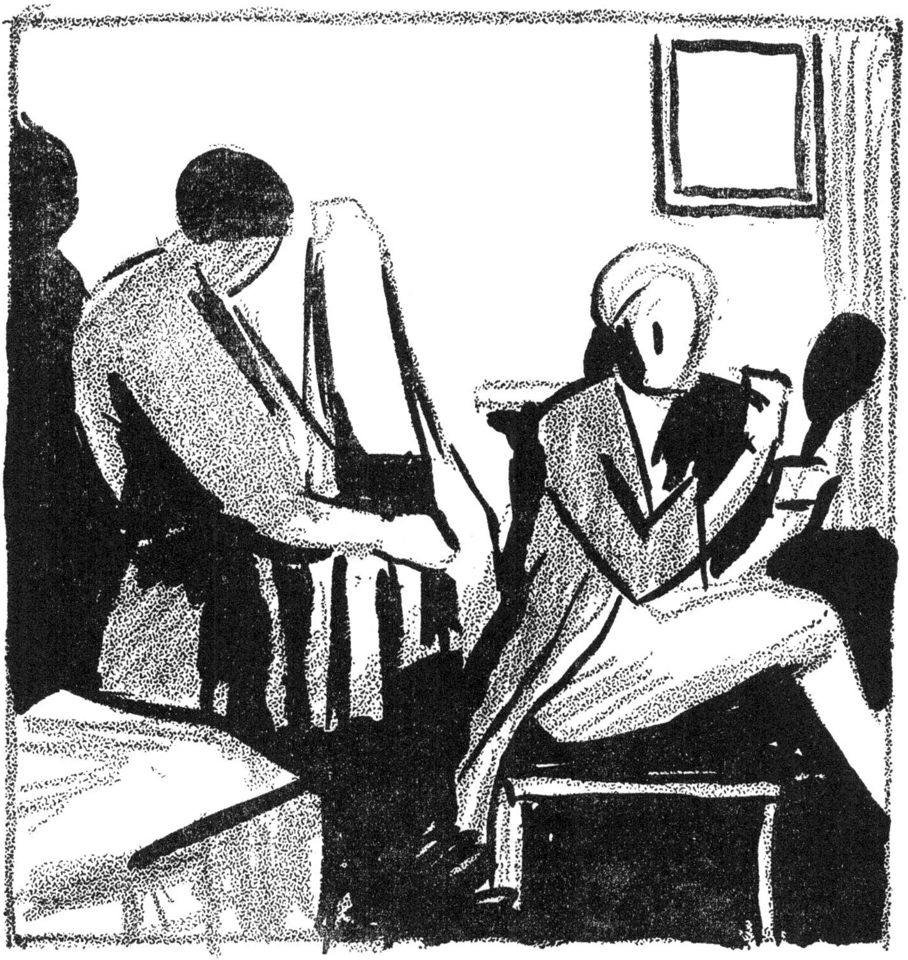

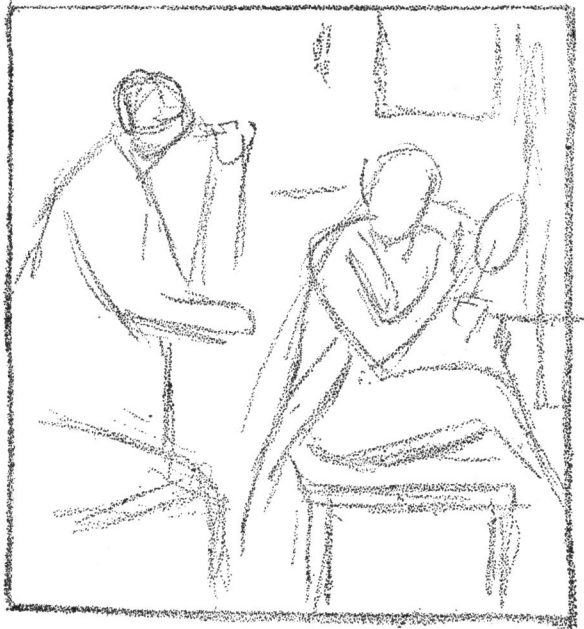

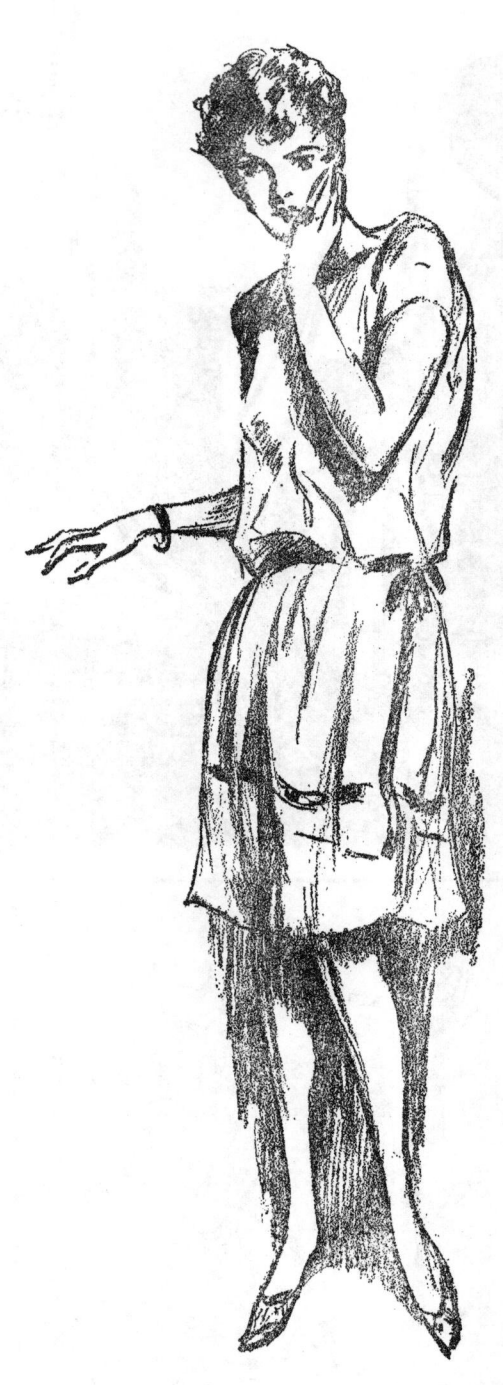

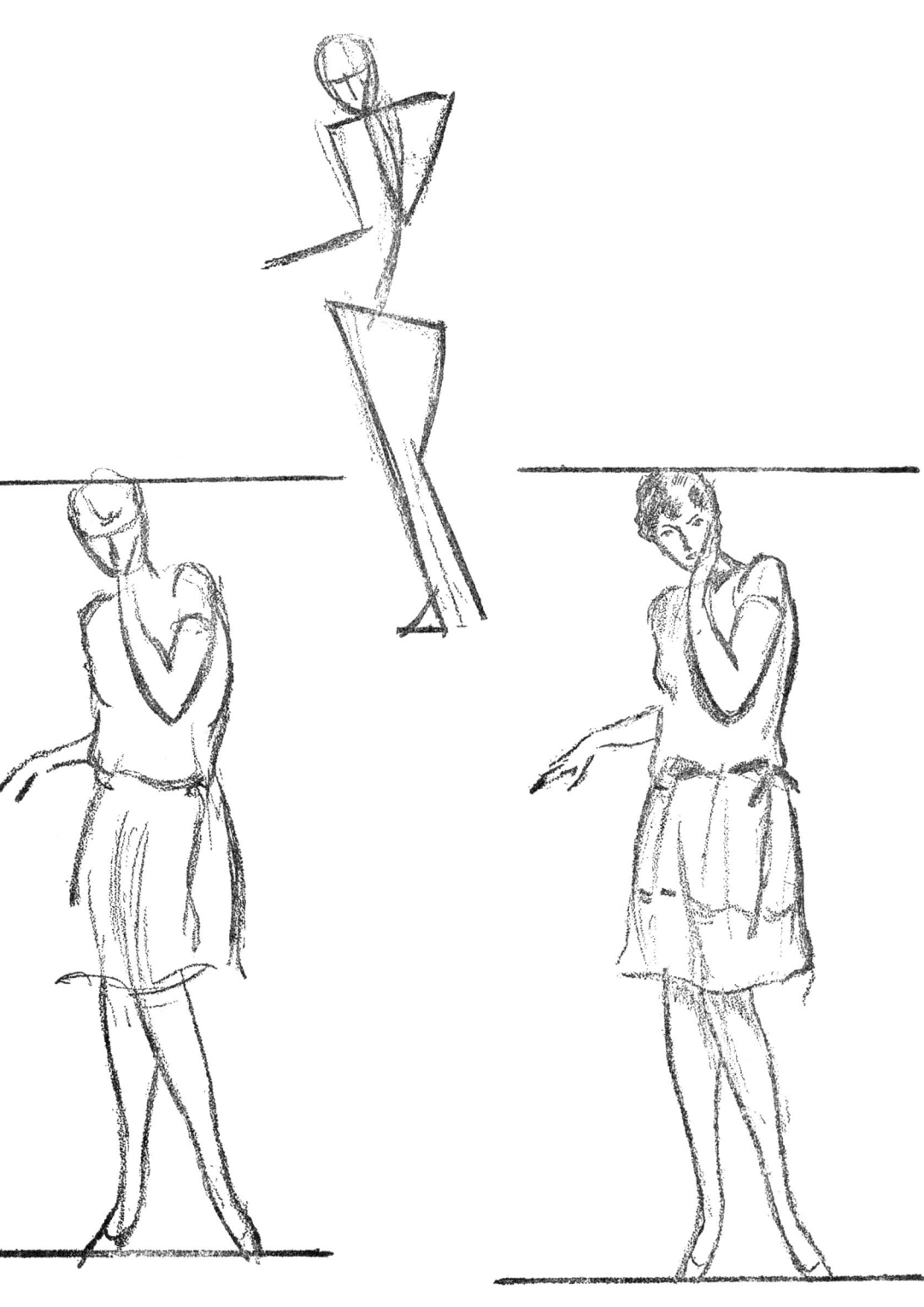

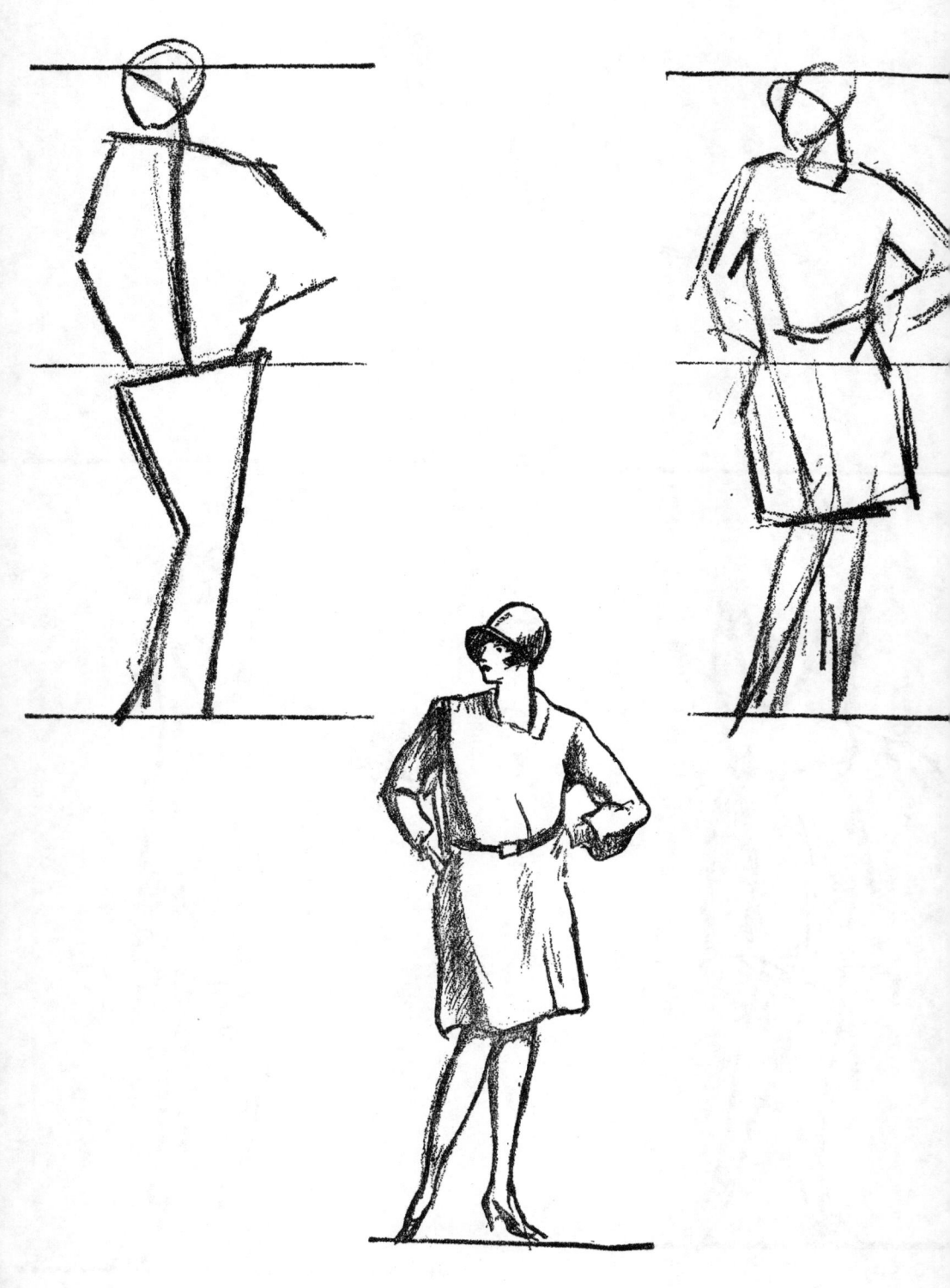

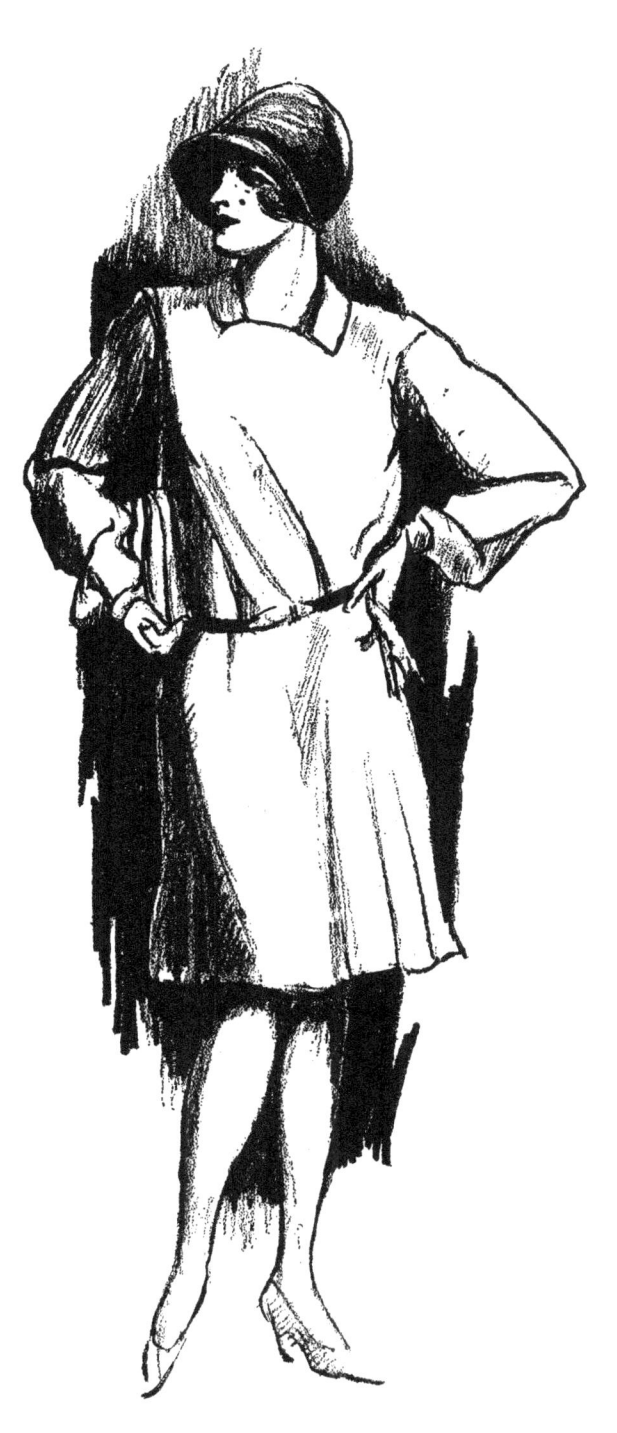

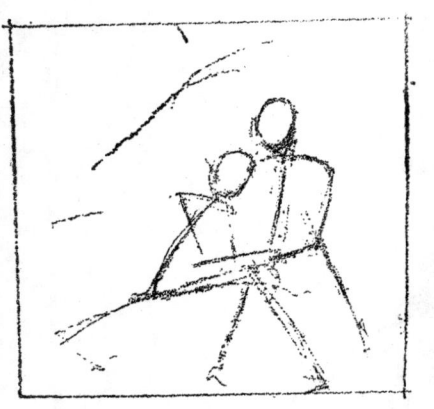
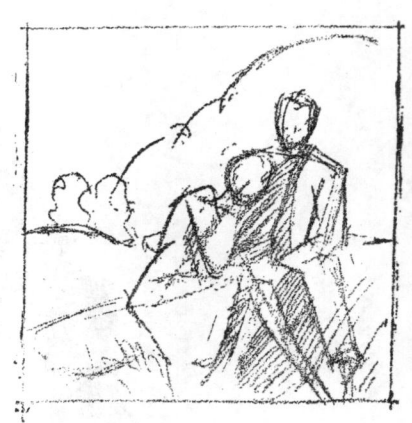

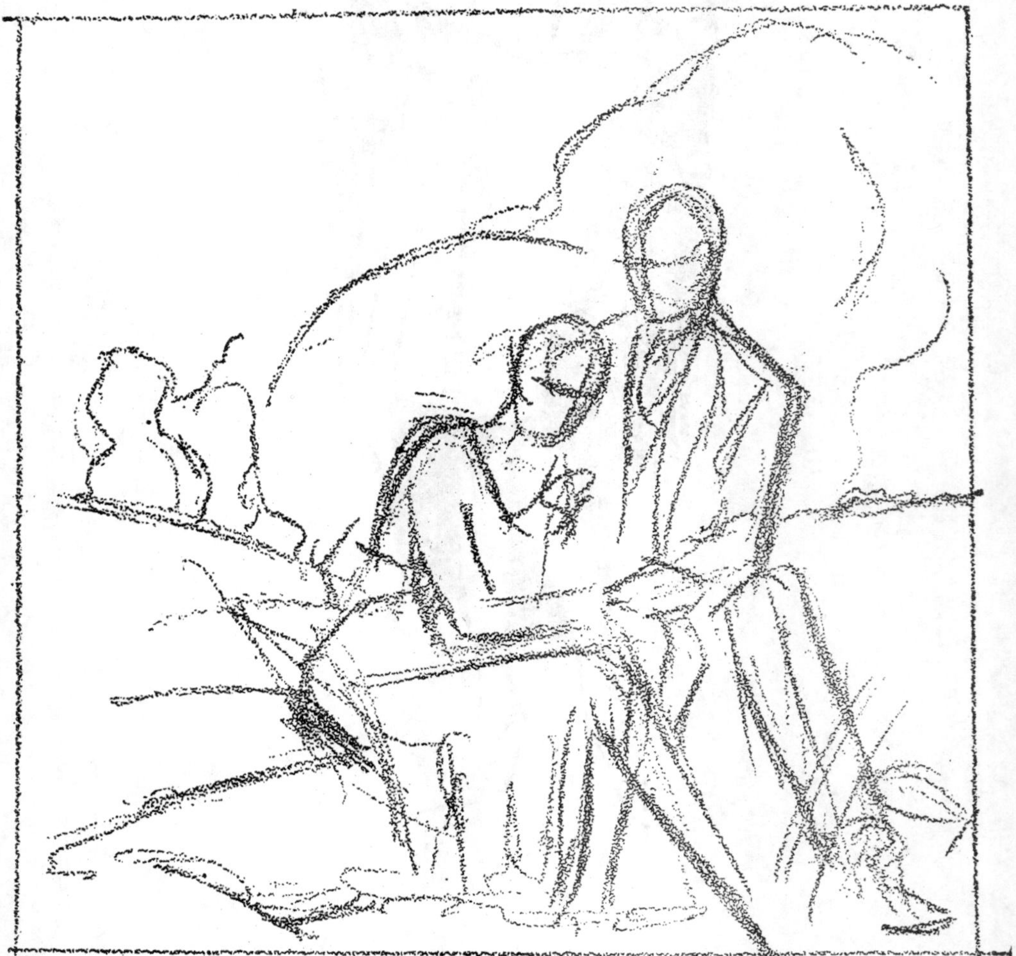

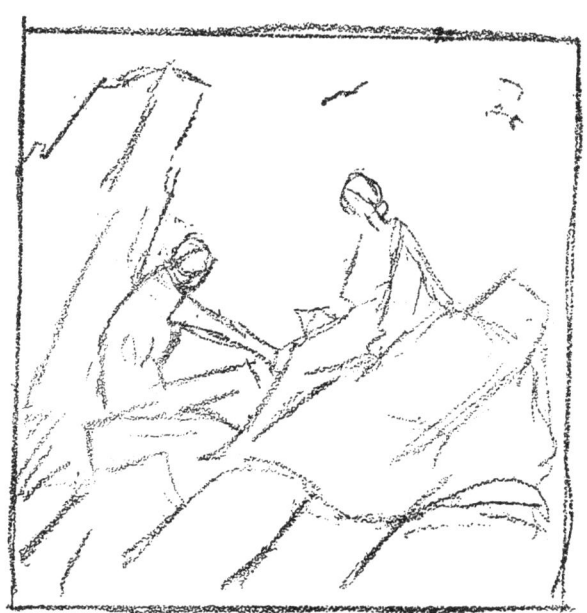

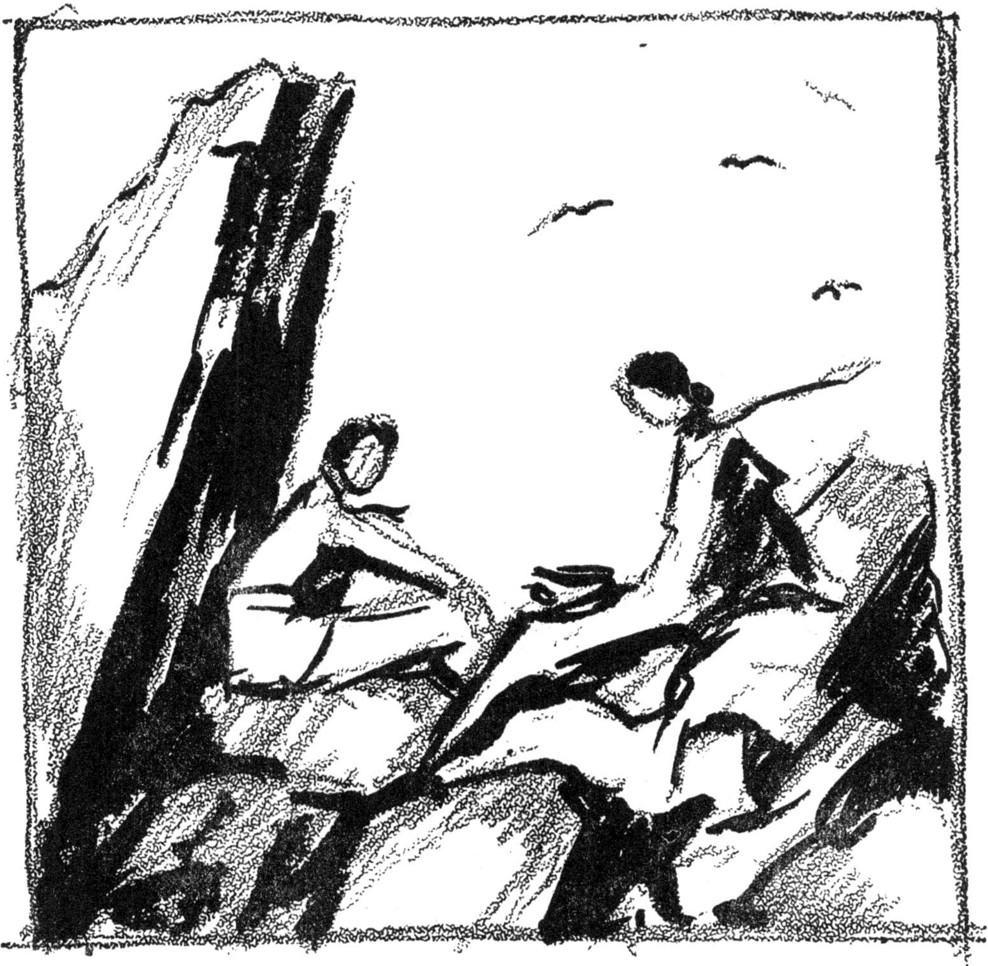

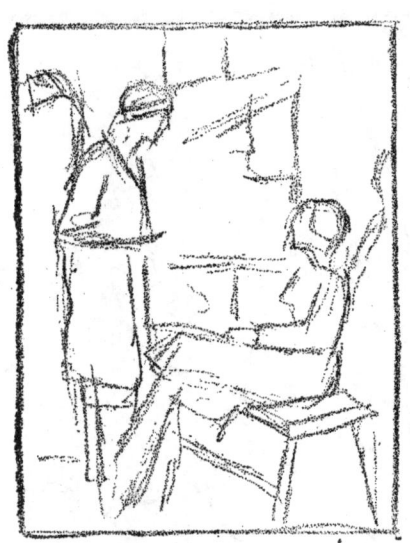

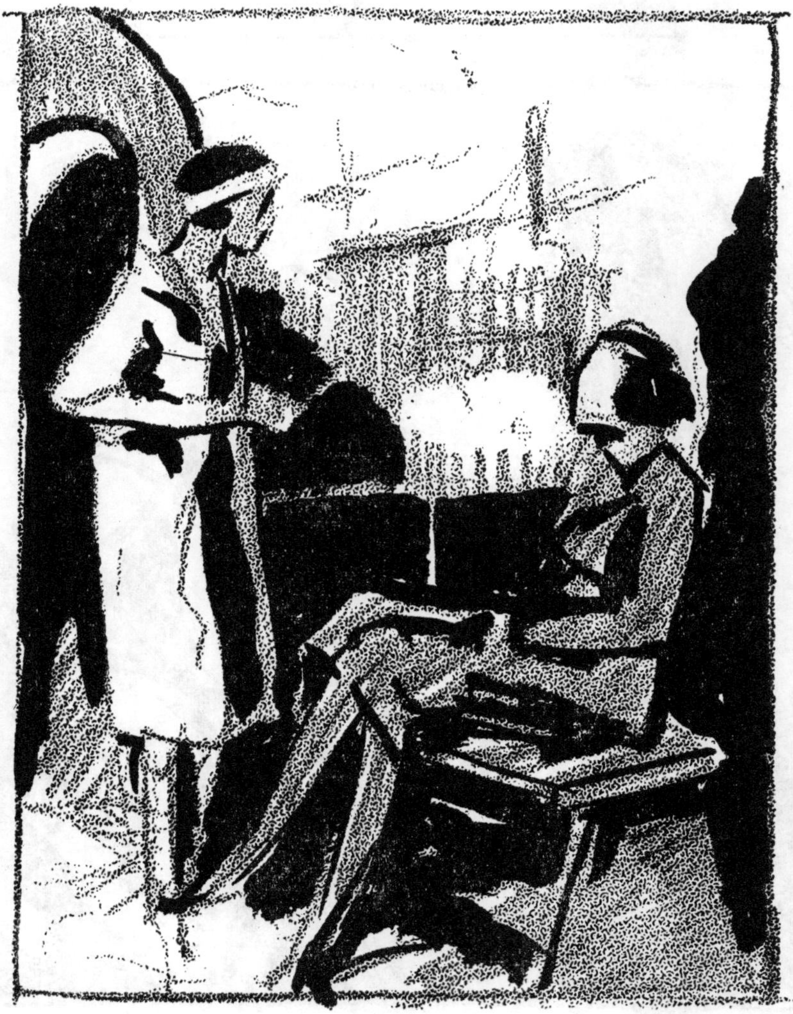

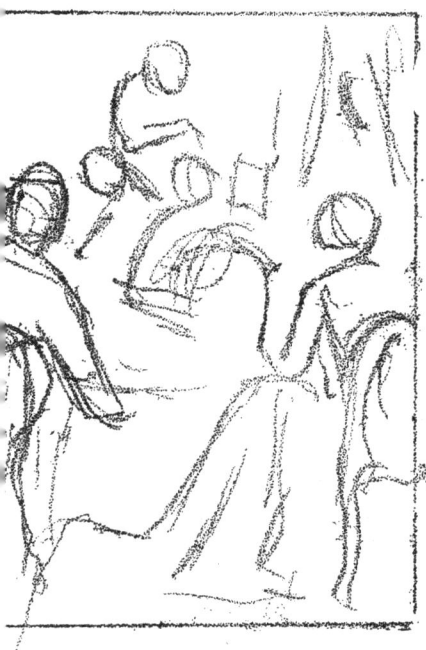

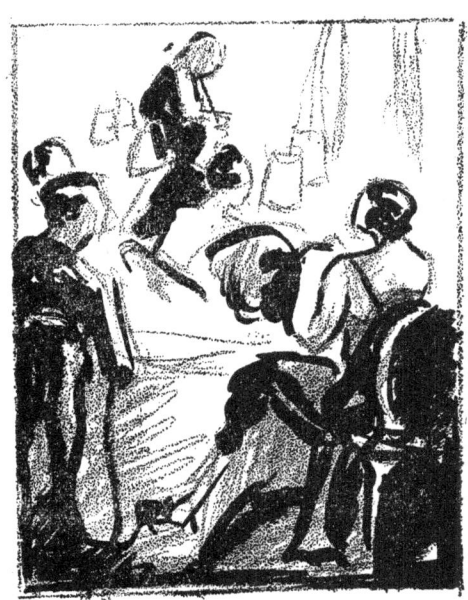

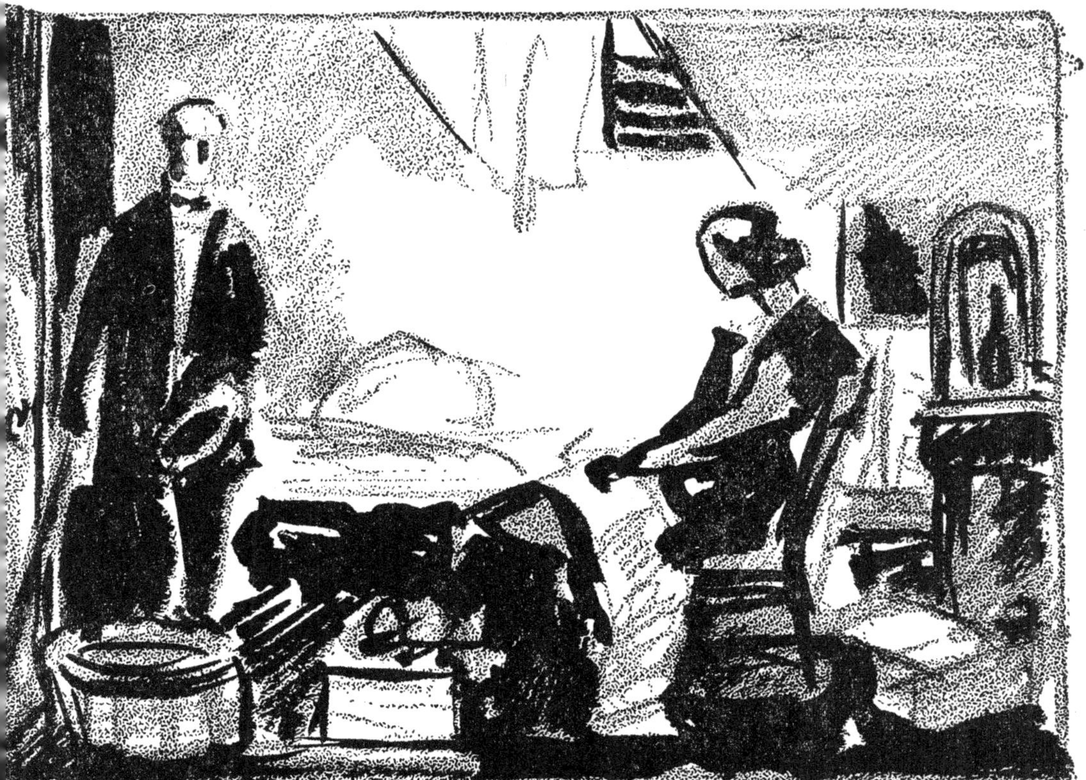

FOLDS

Apart from the actual figure this is the most important study for successful life sketching.

You will notice that nearly all the illustrations are of men's clothes. It may be safely said that if one can manage to master the folds and creases in men's modern clothes you have mastered the chief difficulties of drapery drawing.

Some of you may recall the wonderful drawings of drapery by the old masters, such as Botticelli; fold over fold, crease within crease, all so accurately drawn that the form of the figure beneath and its pose are intensified by the very drapery which covers it. Alas, not an old master nor a new one, but just a quick sketch of folds. Even in this you will see how the folds give the form and pose of the figure; such is the great purpose of folds in a drawing.

The folds of silk are sharp and jagged when compared with those of velvet or similar soft material.

The thicker the cloth the larger and bolder the creases.

A thin material unless very hard cannot stand up in big folds, but breaks into many little ones.

It is good practice to make studies from different materials dropped carelessly over the arm of a chair.

Creases are caused by a crumpling or a hanging, by a slackness or a tautness. In slackness the creases are jumbled, of no general direction, and are short and wide.

Never draw a crease unless you have decided what type it is, whether crumpled, hanging, or taut; what is its length, breadth and direction. A badly drawn crease destroys the very action and form which it should emphasize.

It is splendid practice to make quick studies, from good photographs in periodicals; taking care to find out the reason for every crease and to draw the most important ones first.

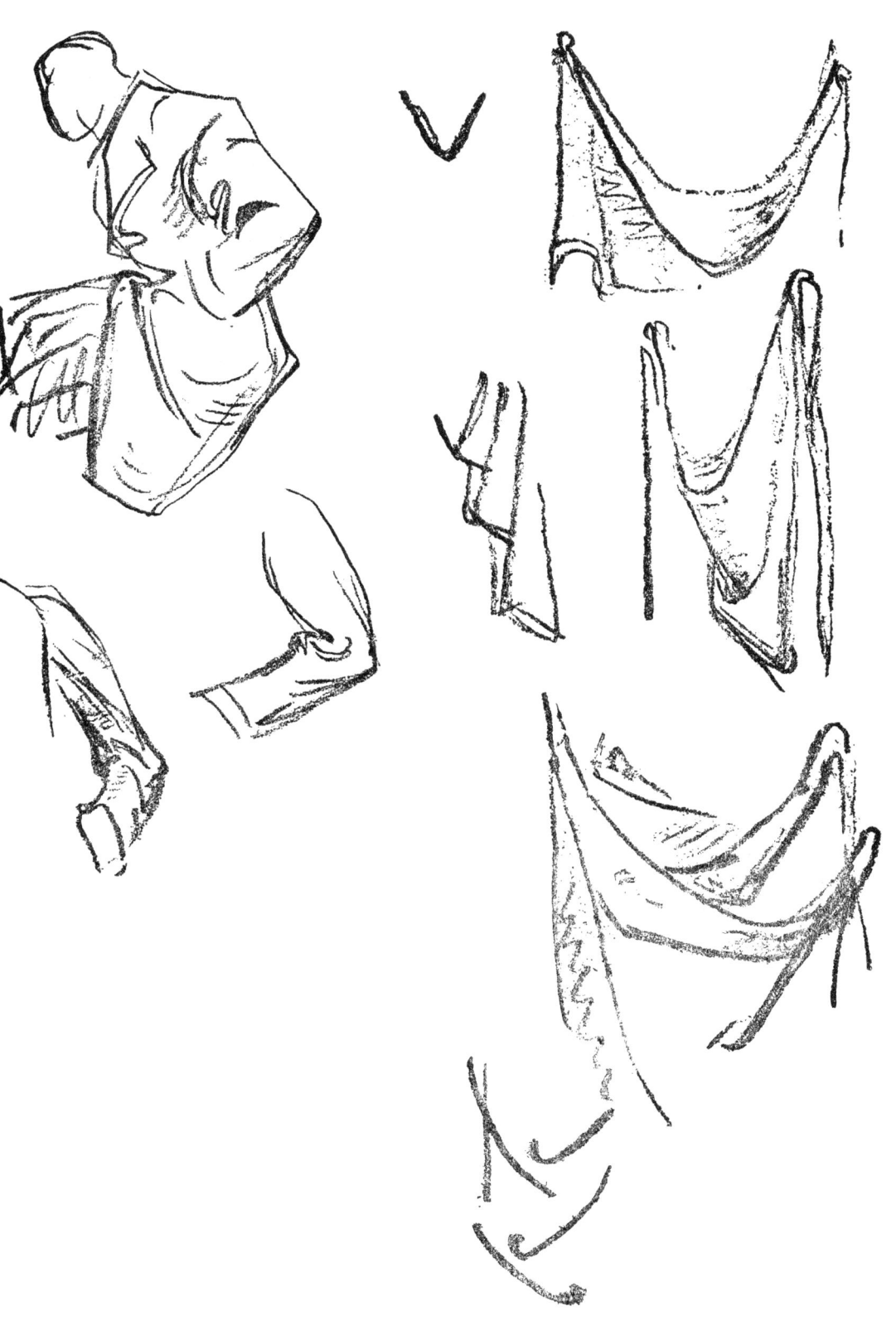

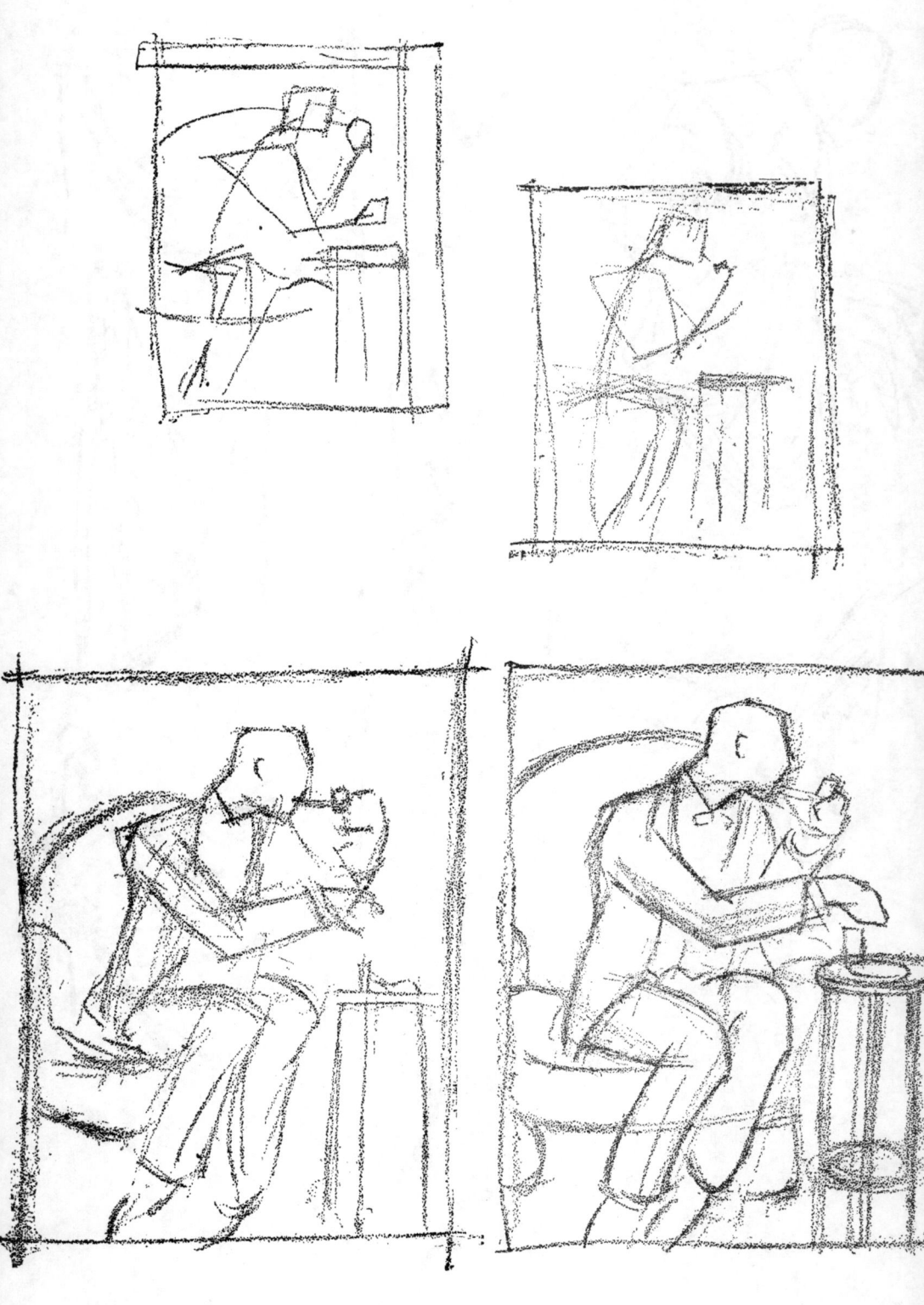

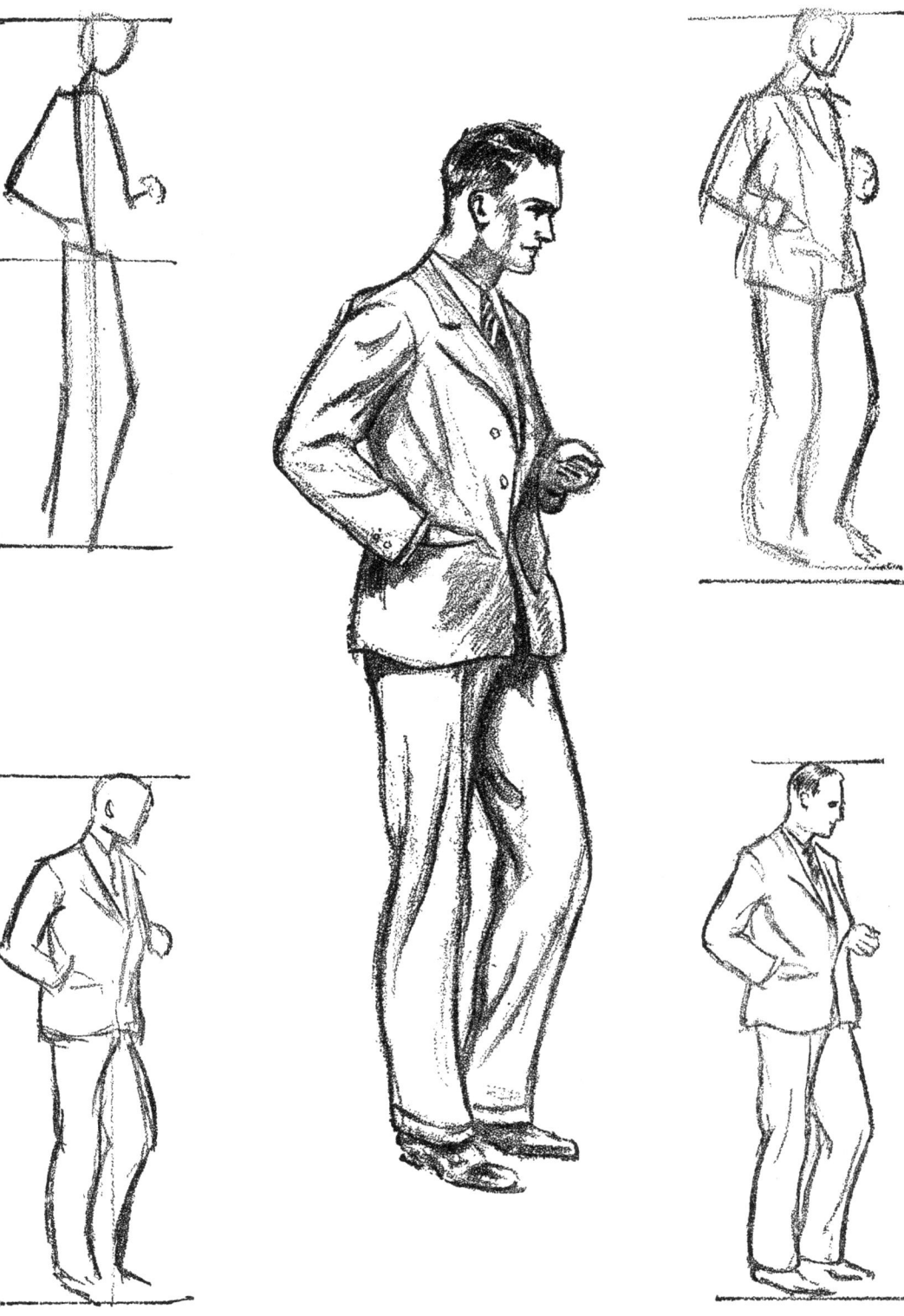

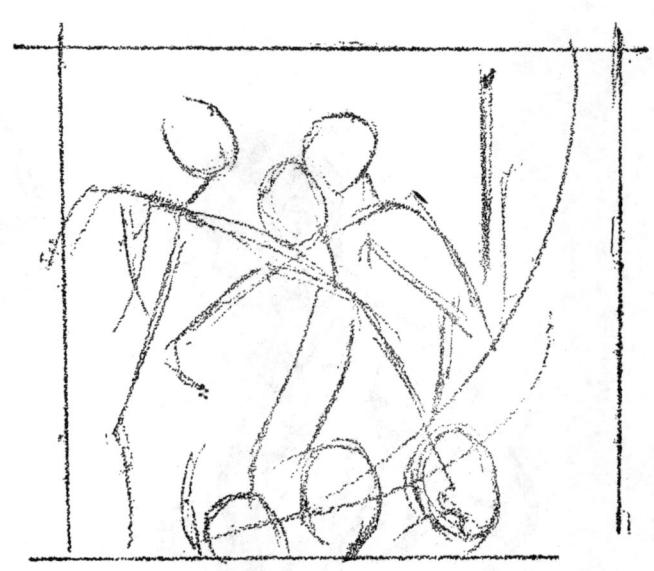

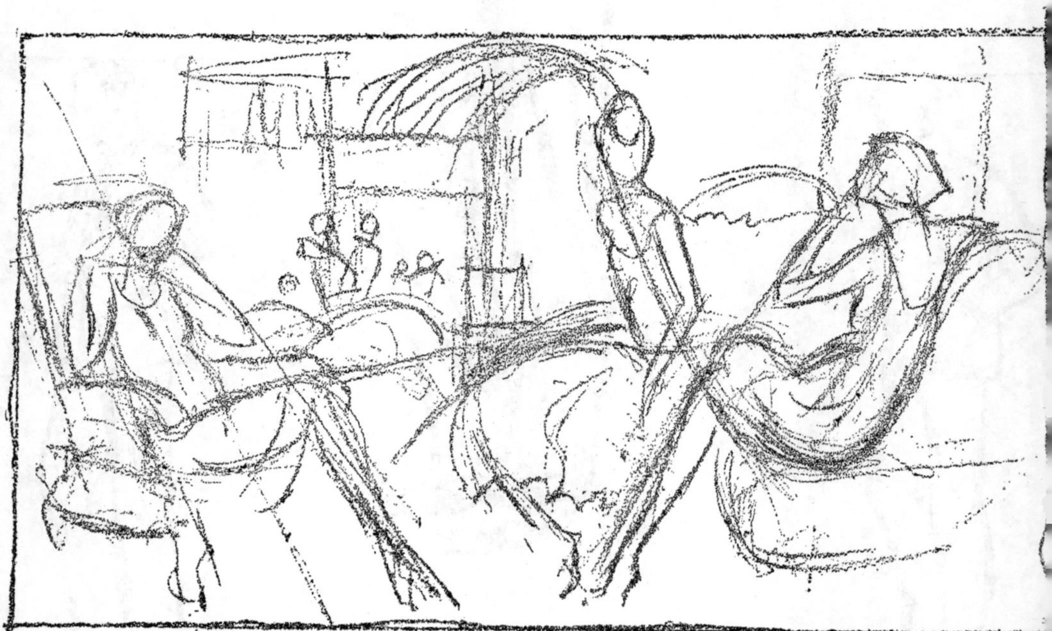

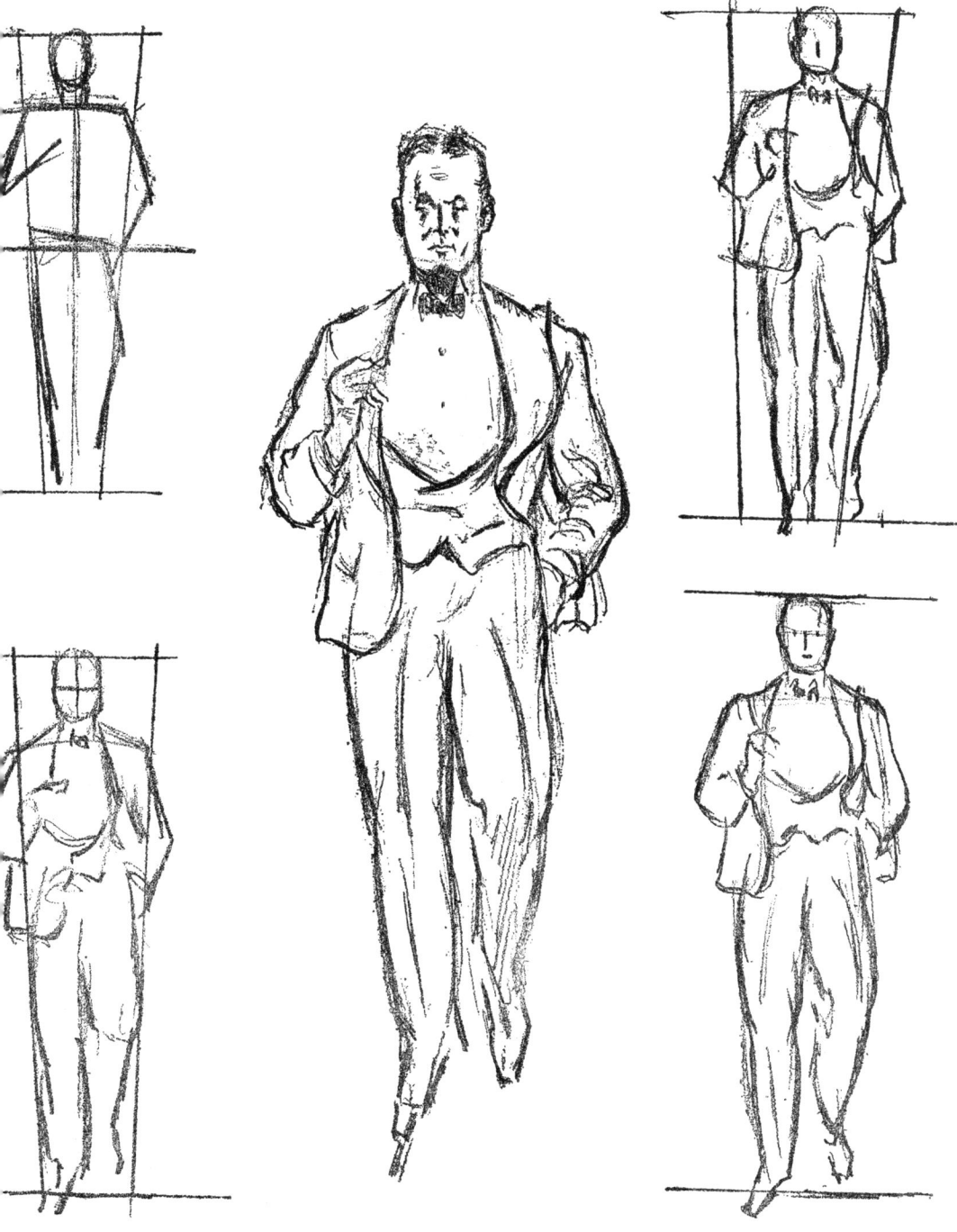

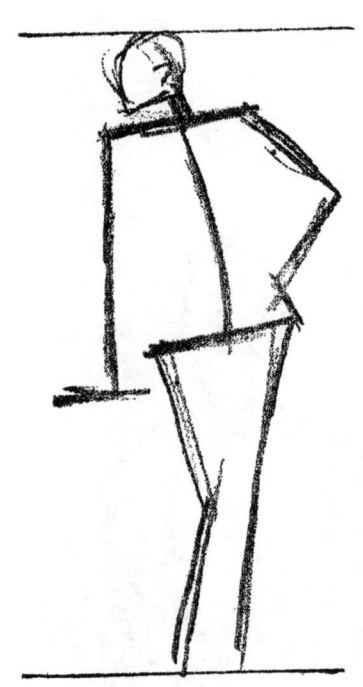

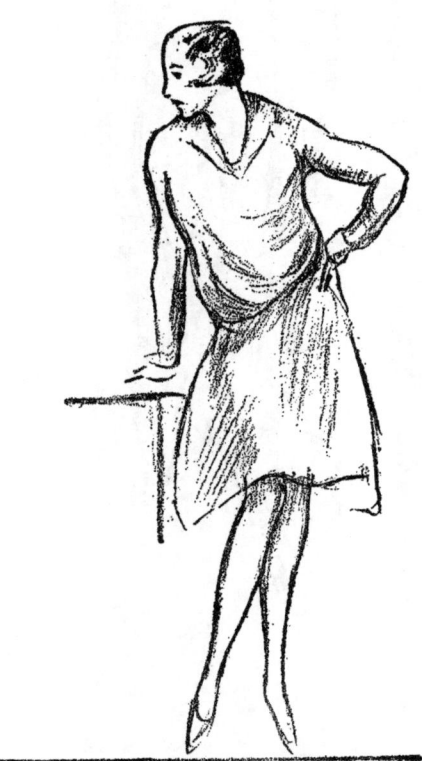

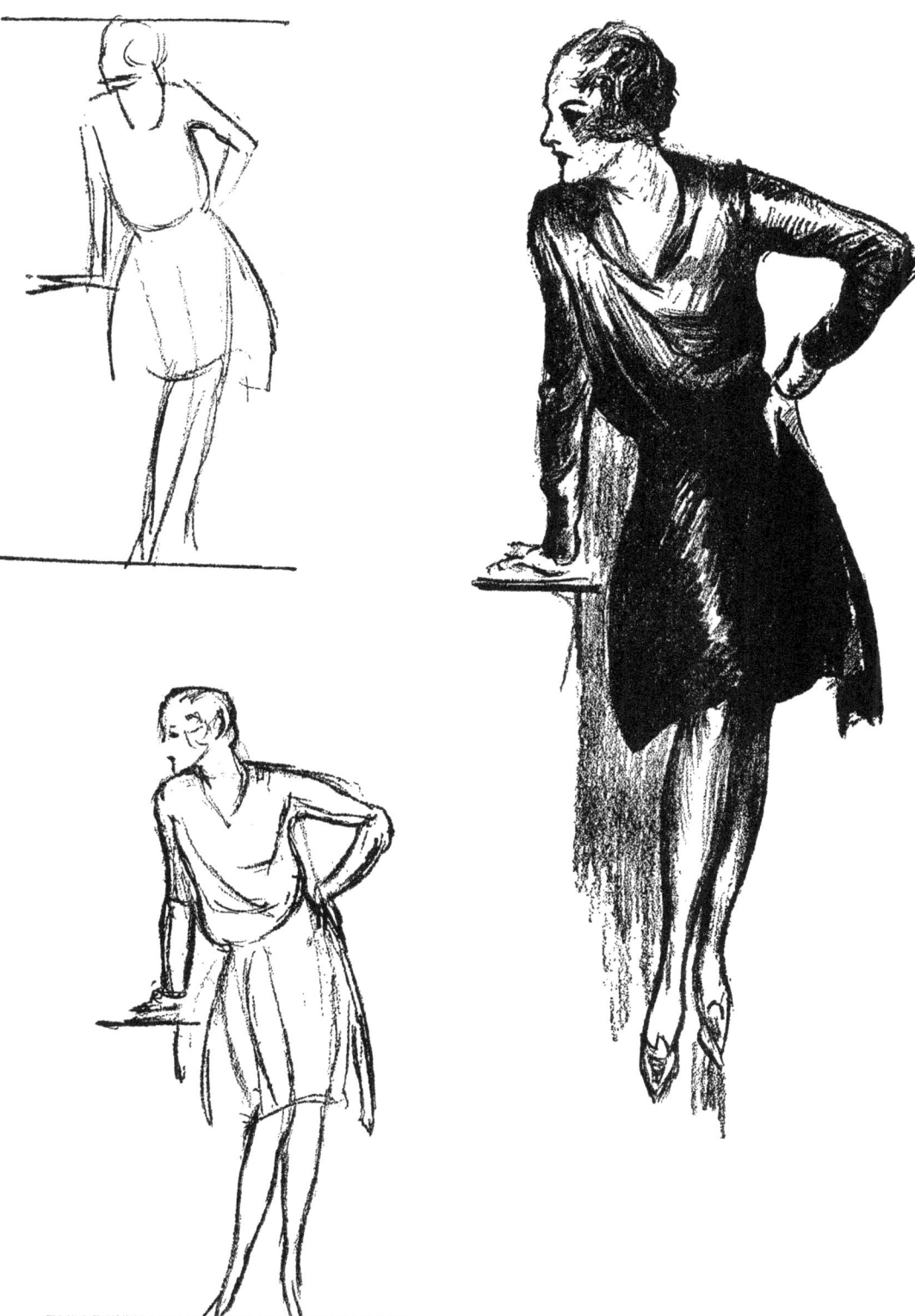

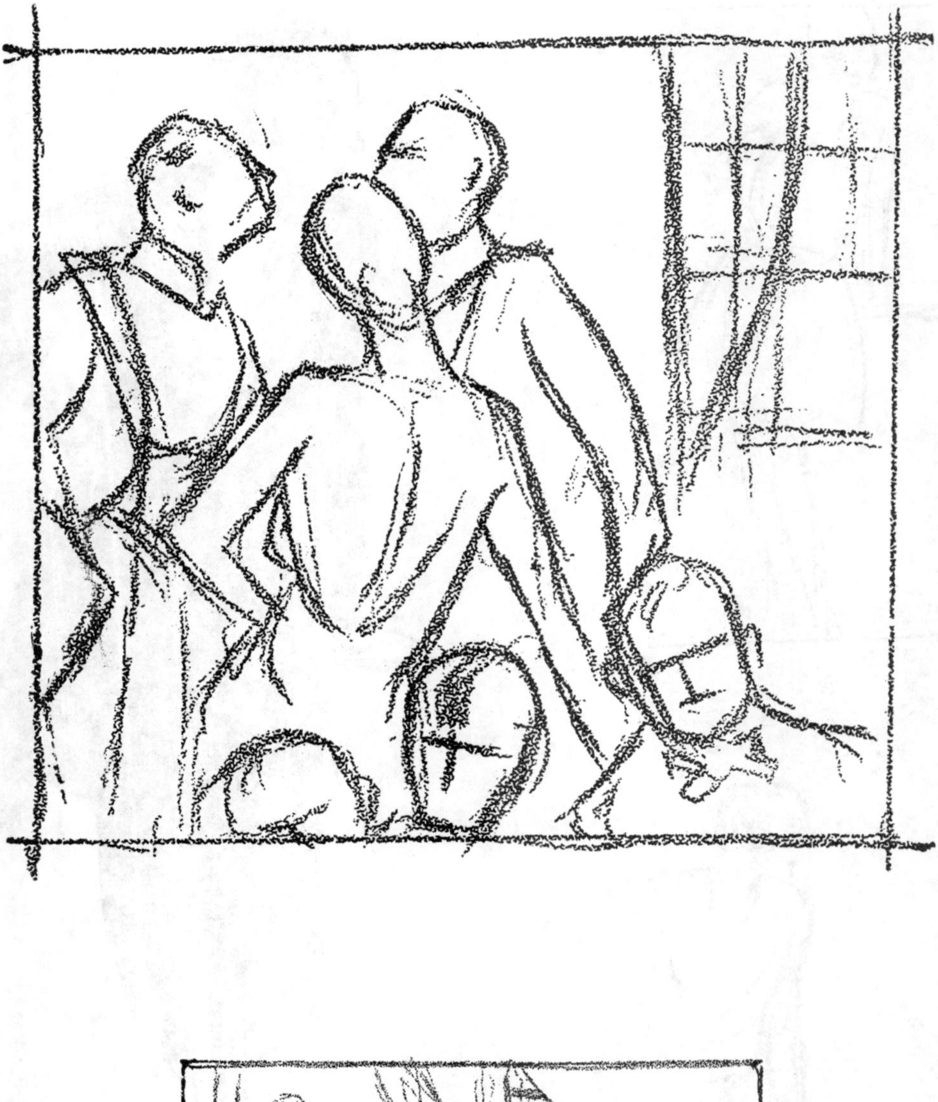

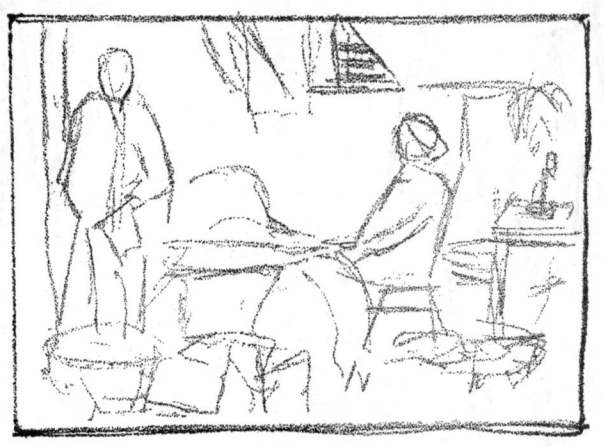

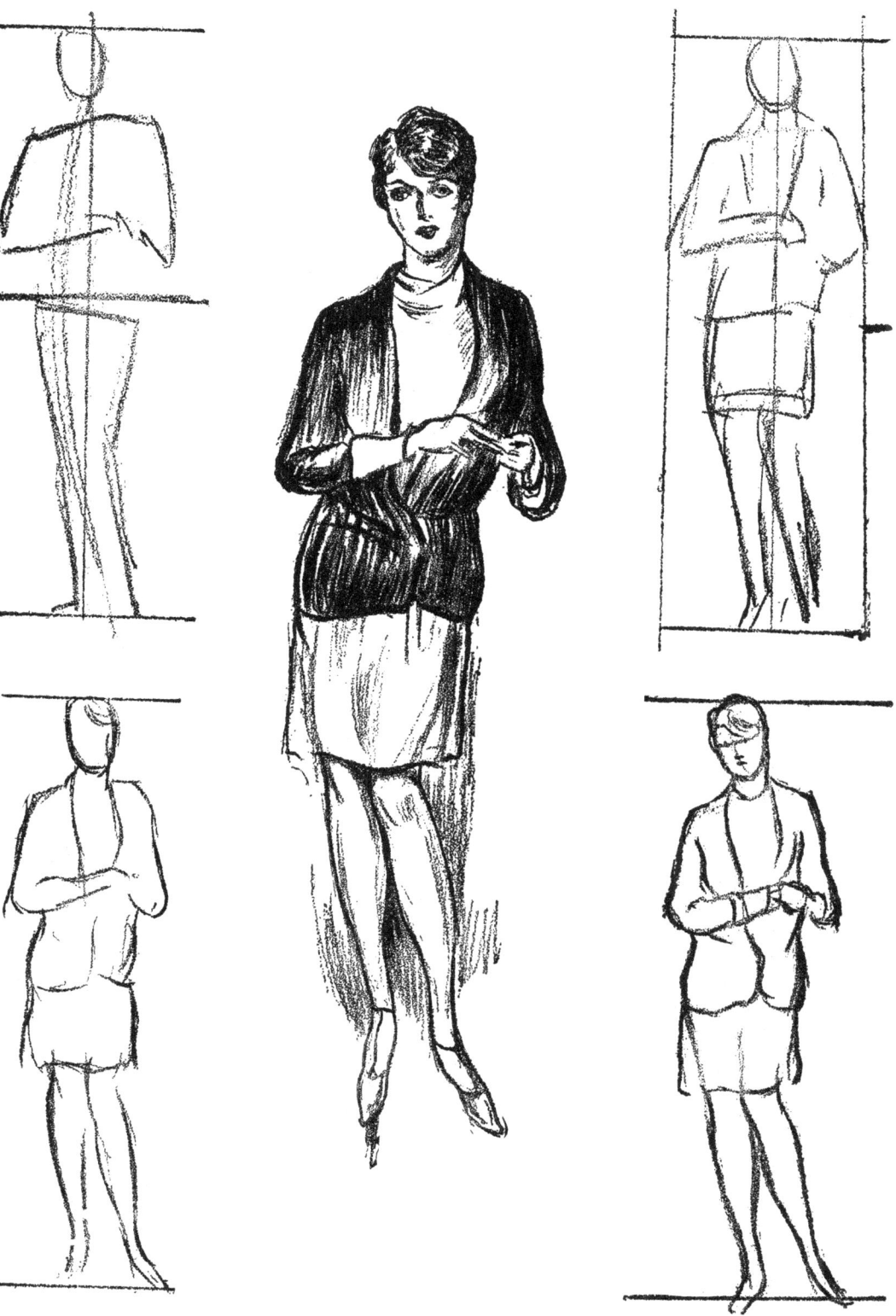

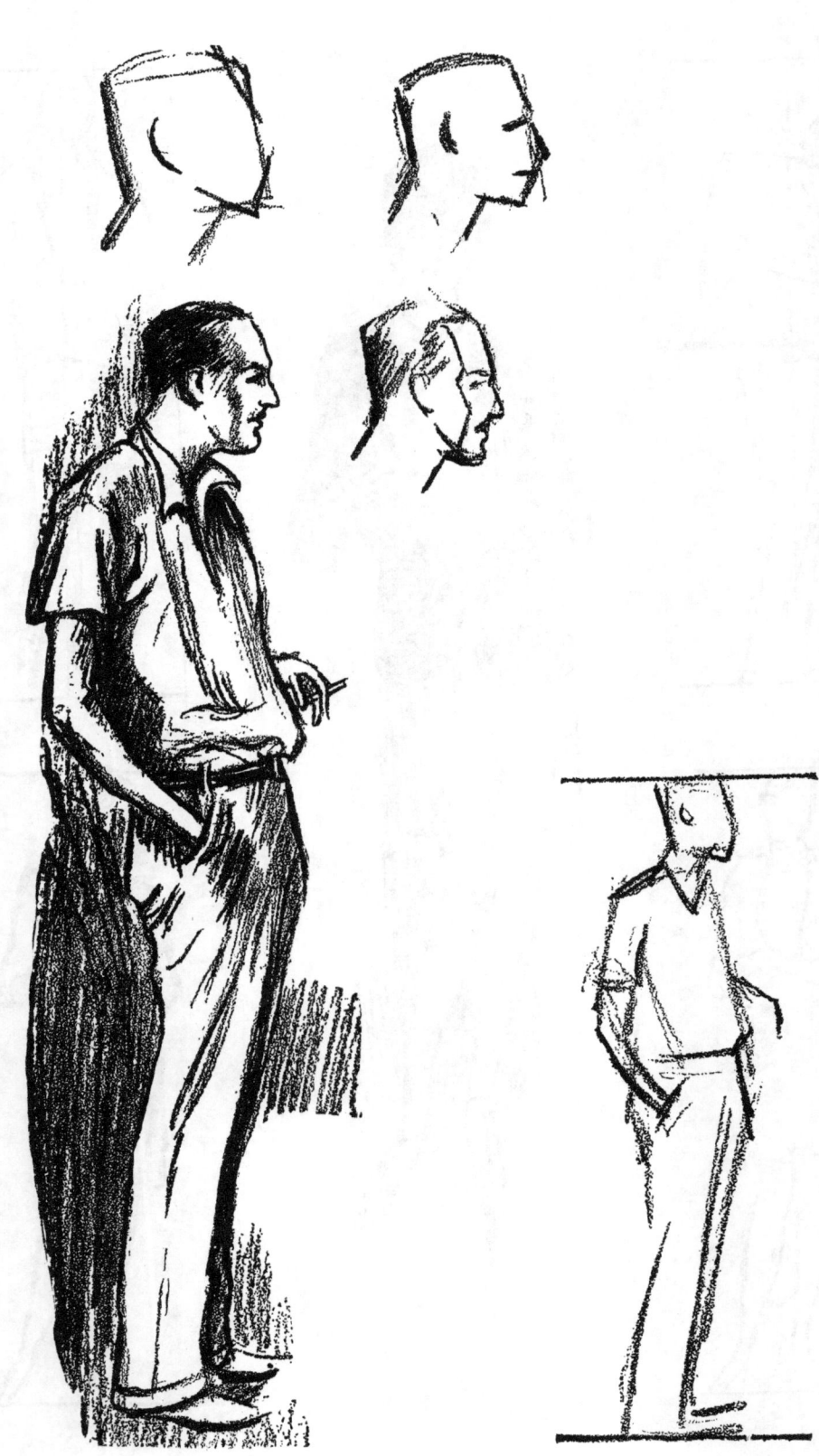

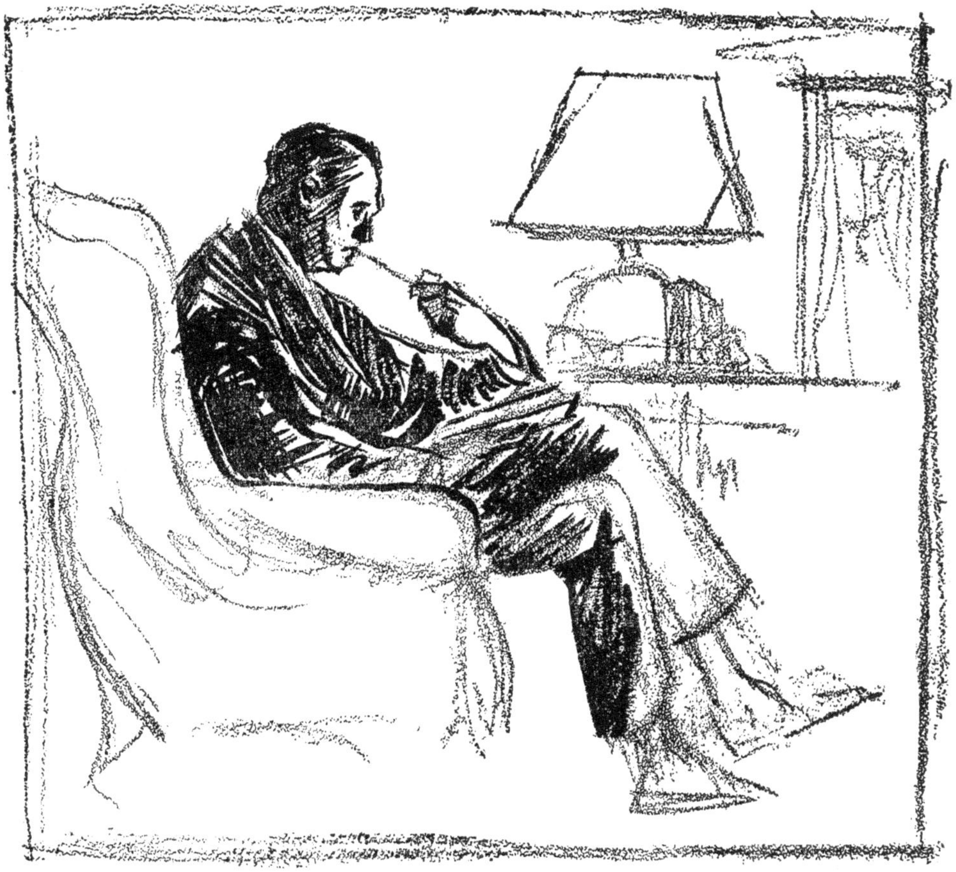

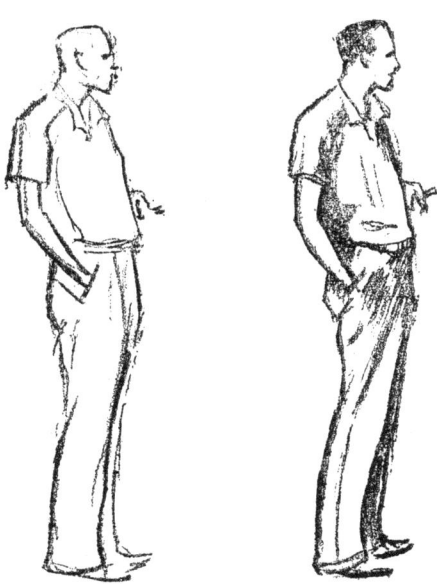

RHYTHM

The consciousness or idea of rhythm can not be traced to any period, or to any artist or group of artists. We know that in 1349 a group of Florentine artists formed a society for the study of the chemistry of colors, the mathematics of composition, etc., and that among these studies was the science of motion. But rhythm was not invented. It has been the measured motion of the Universe since the beginning of time. There is rhythm in the movement of the sea and tides, stars and planets, trees and grasses, clouds and thistledown. It is a part of all animal and plant life. It is the movement of uttered words, expressed in their accented and unaccented syllables, and in the grouping and pauses of speech. Both poetry and music are the embodiment, in appropriate rhythmical sound, of beautiful thought, imagination or emotion. Without rhythm there could be no poetry or music. In drawing and painting there is rhythm in outline, color, light and shade.

The slow, continuous moving picture has given us a new appreciation of rhythm in all visible movement.

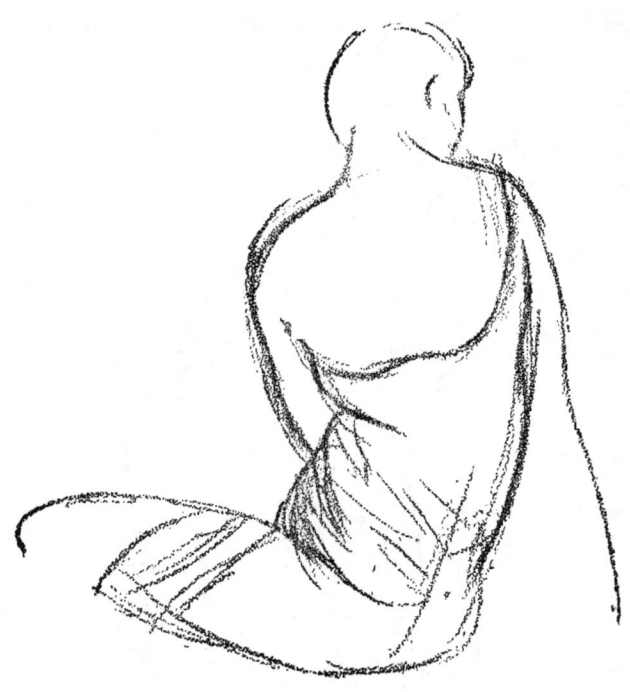

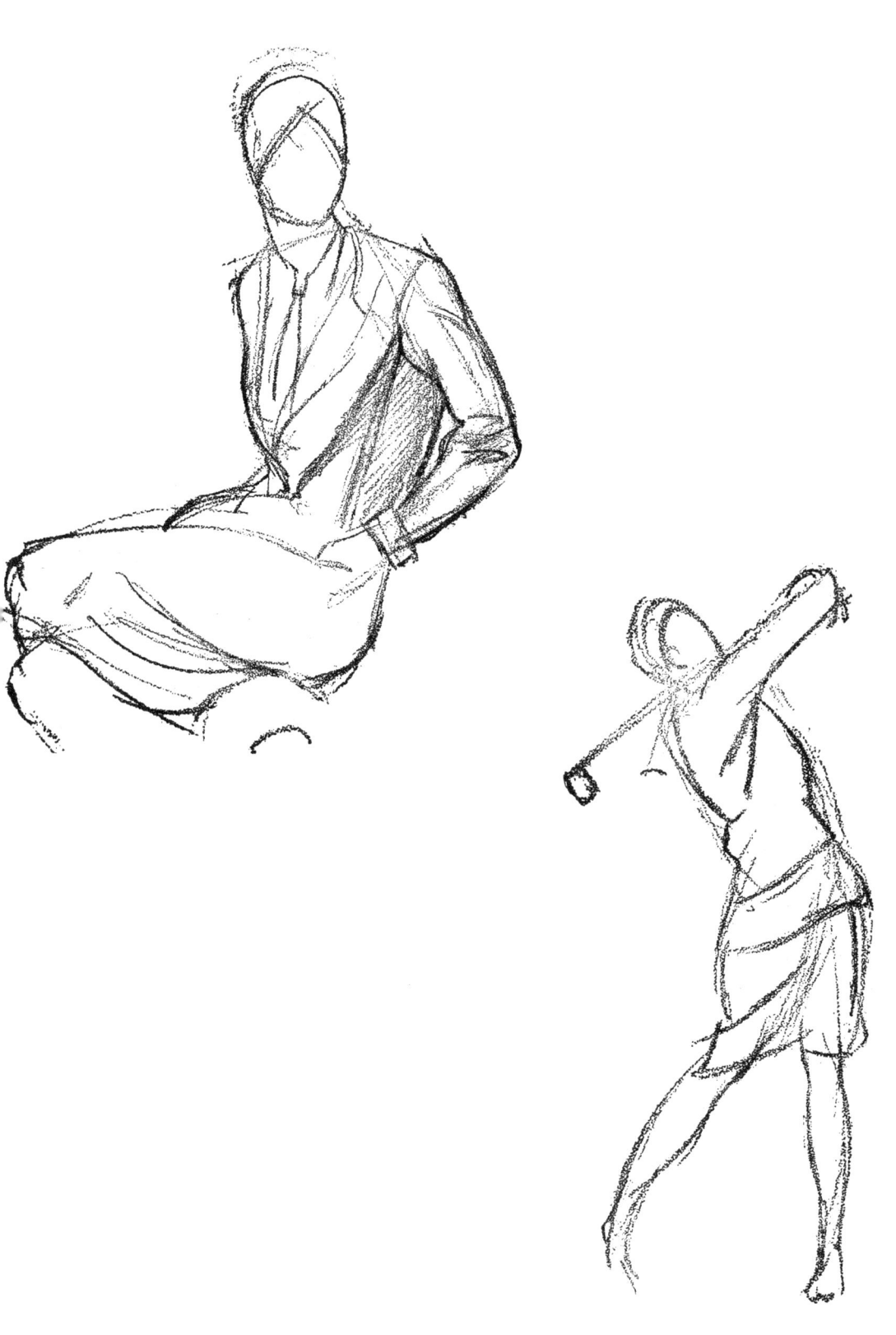

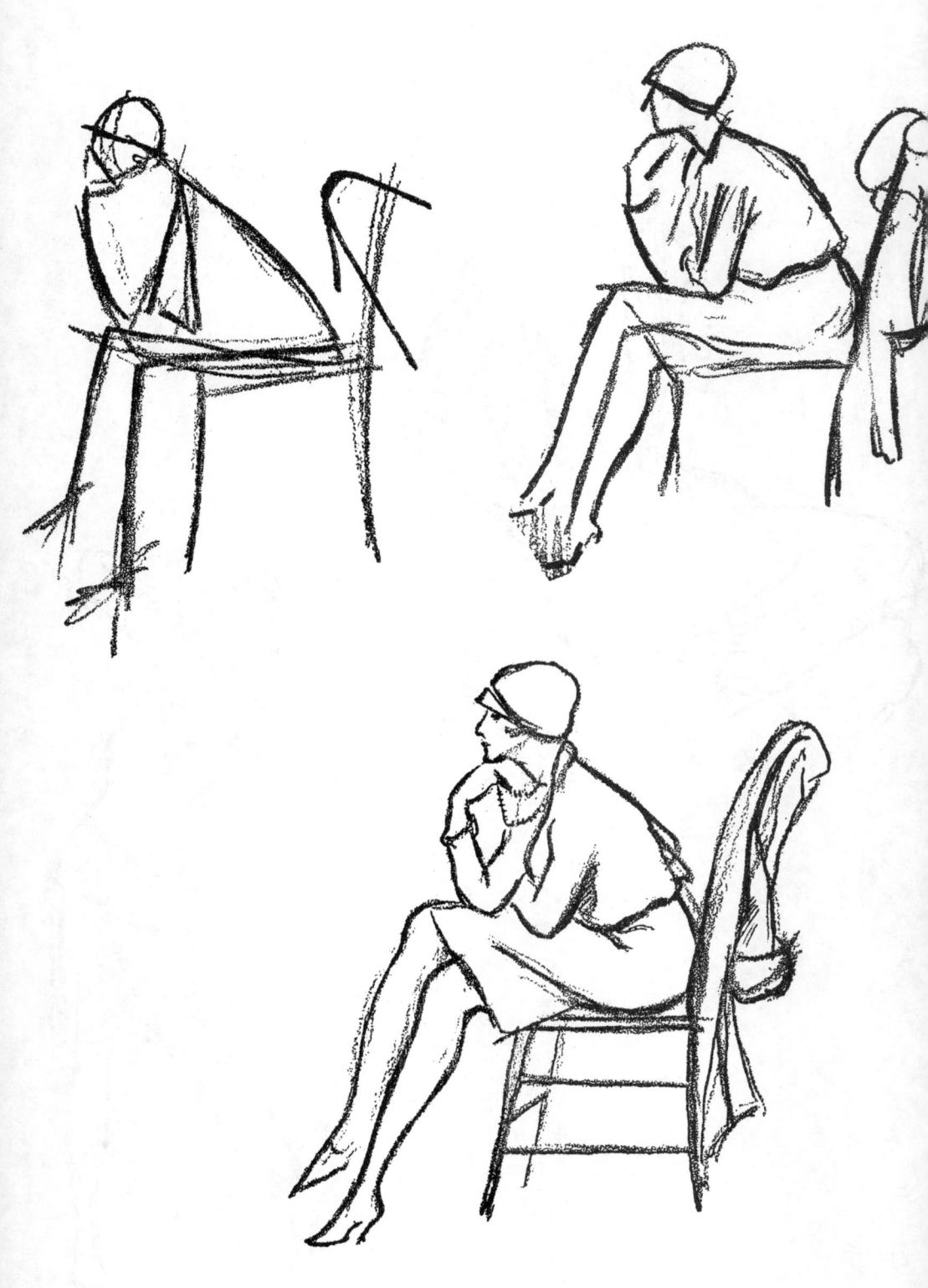

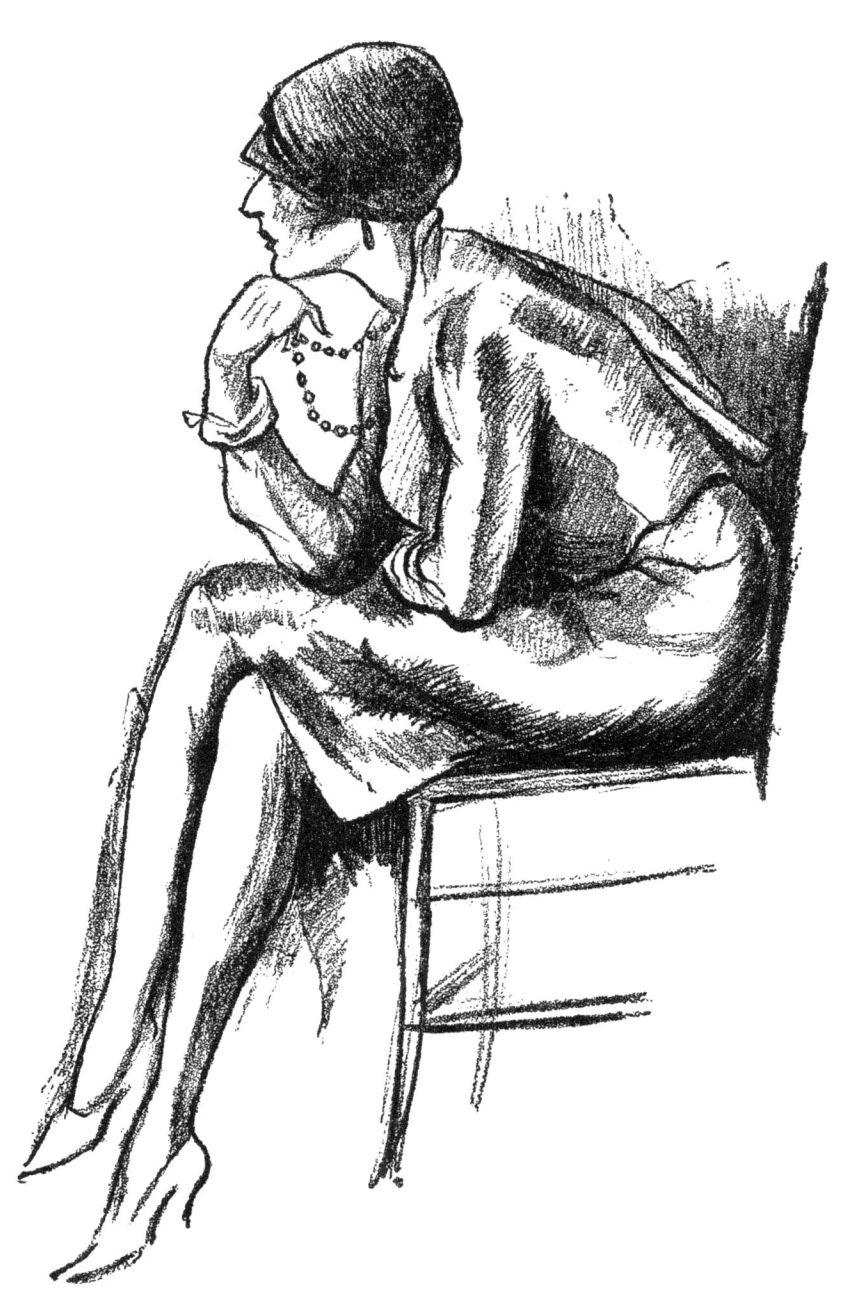

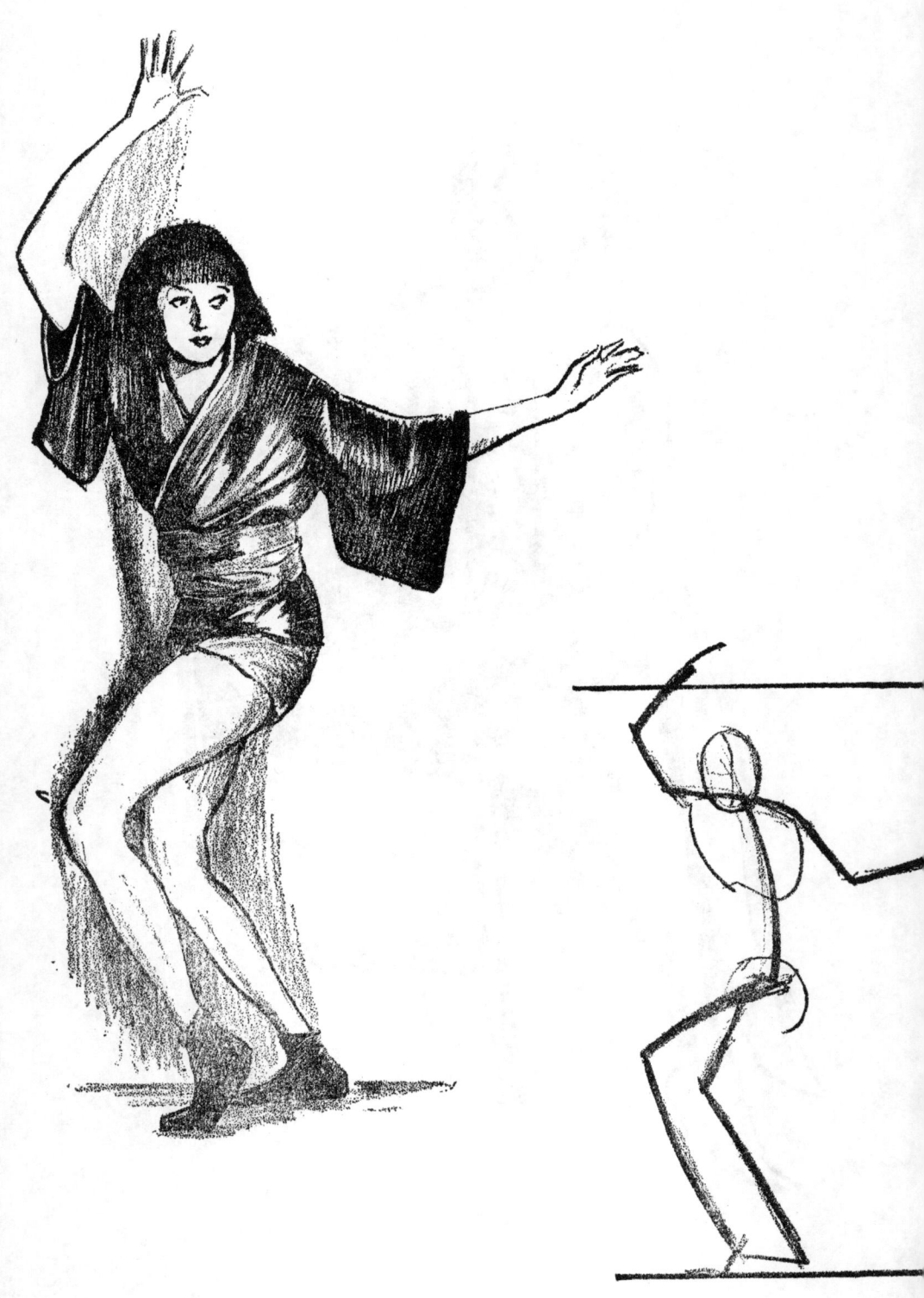

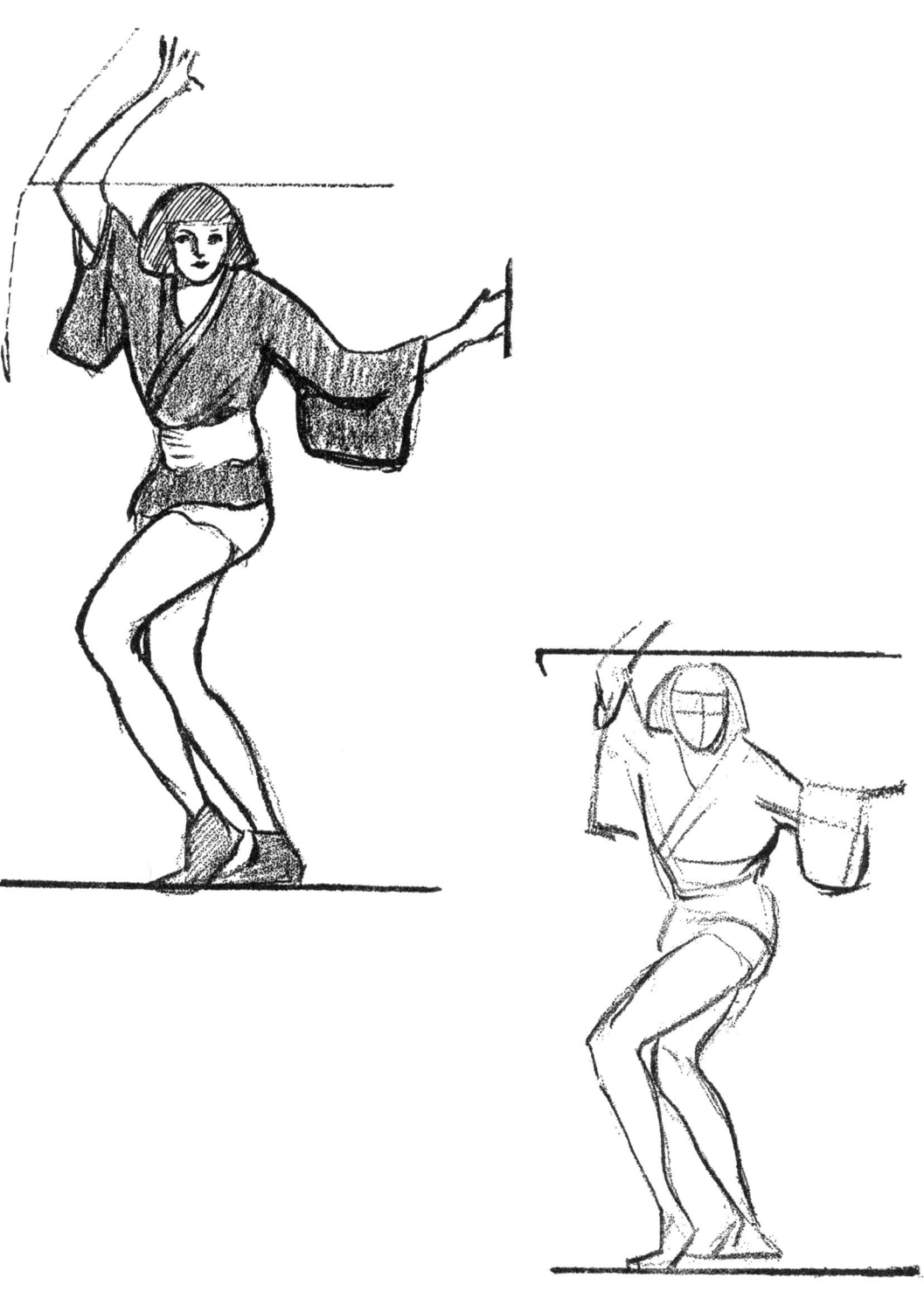

SKETCHING

Construct a simple rectangle and pose your model side-view with a strong light playing upon the front of the figure. Draw the figure as before, using only the big simple shapes. When you are sure it is as correct as you can possibly get it, get your figure in proportion, action, etc. Stop and study it for a while.

Observe the head, the front of the face, where it turns the corner and the side begins. See how that side is darker—this dark suggesting to you solidity. The so called dark or shadow is nothing in itself. It would not be there only for the form beneath it. Its only value is to designate the turning of a corner.

Look at the torso, the same thing occurs—the arms—the legs.

On your drawing decide where these edges are and darken the side away from the light.

Use only a light tone in the beginning—there is always time for heavy darks.

Make many drawings this way, using more figures, furniture, and other objects. Move the light around to fit your own ideas.

Form gives life to your figures and solidity can best be gotten by the use of light and dark.

Copying shadows will never help you. They have no value as shadows, only as the darkened side of an object to show where form "turns the corner" so to speak.

Watch the line of movement that runs through your figures—keep them alive.

Character may be secured in the use of simple lines,

Note the fit of the costume,

The rightness of things,

The attitude of arm and hand and its simplicity and the use of simple wrinkles.

Use wrinkles to show form, and disregard the others entirely.

Note the simple suggestion of the environment in which the figure moves.

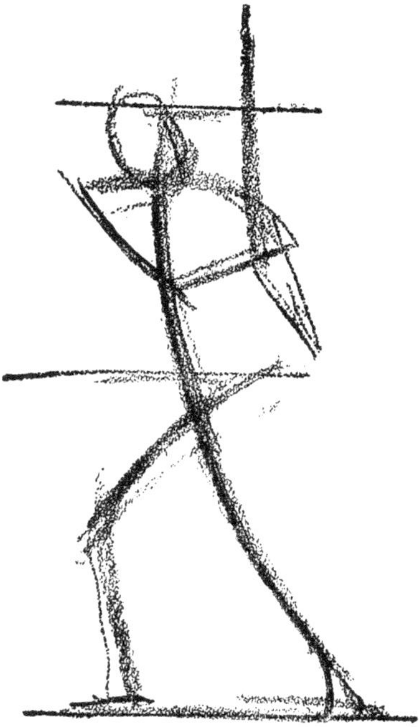

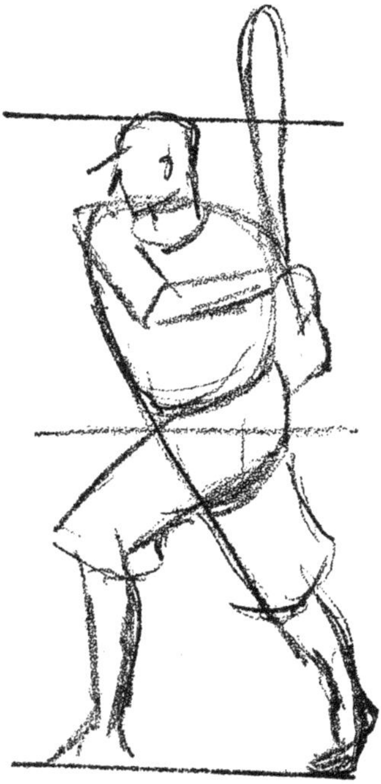

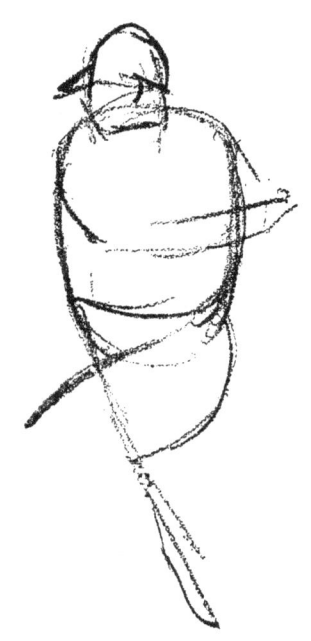
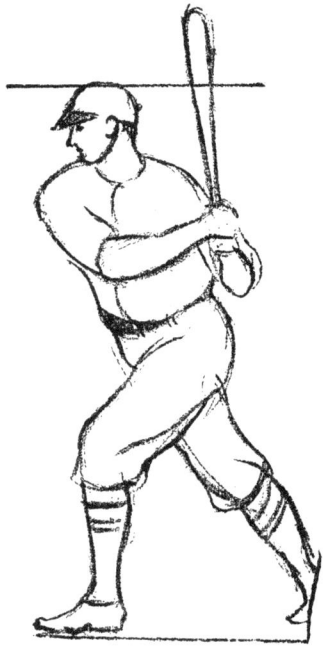

Whenever you go into the park or whenever you are in a public conveyance, sketch. Carry paper and pencil with you at all times. And use them. Don't be self-conscious, sketch what you see.

The sense of sketching creates a certain element of action in your drawings that you cannot get any other way.

Endless subjects are available. Park benches are always crowded with interesting characters. Make your sketches quickly, do not stop with one sketch, keep making them and before long you will find that you will get a great amount of detail and the suggestion of detail into your drawing with a fewer number of lines. Try and sketch people who have some unusually noticeable characteristic, either the way they are dressed or sketch them as a character subject. You very seldom see a sketch that is unusual that does not stir you to action.

Use your imagination and no matter what the result may be it will be extremely better progress for you than to have copied someone else's drawing.

Never draw anything without an idea, there is human interest to be found in every subject. Just to draw something is not the sort of practice that will help your progress.

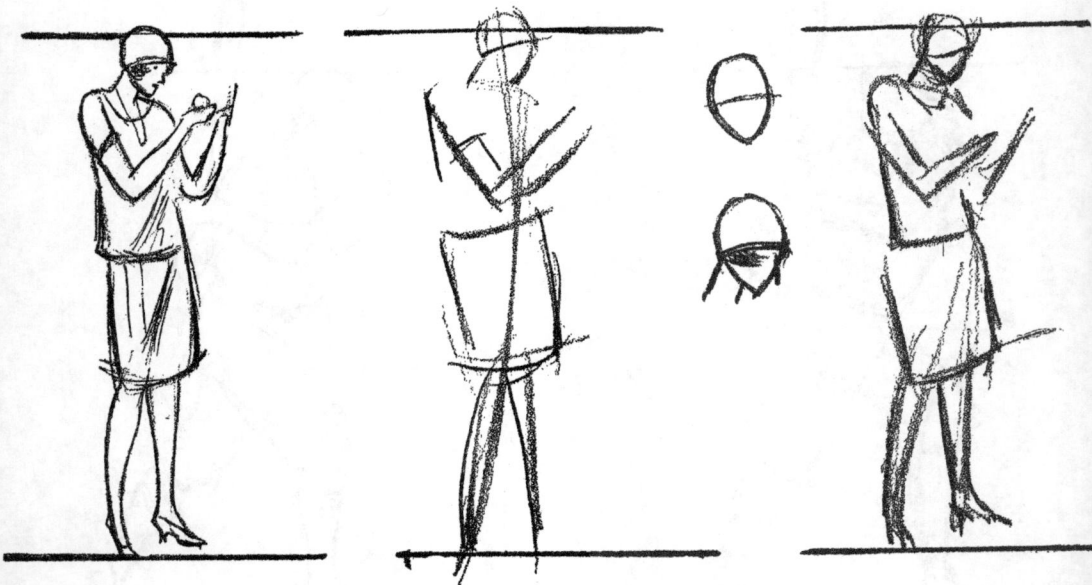

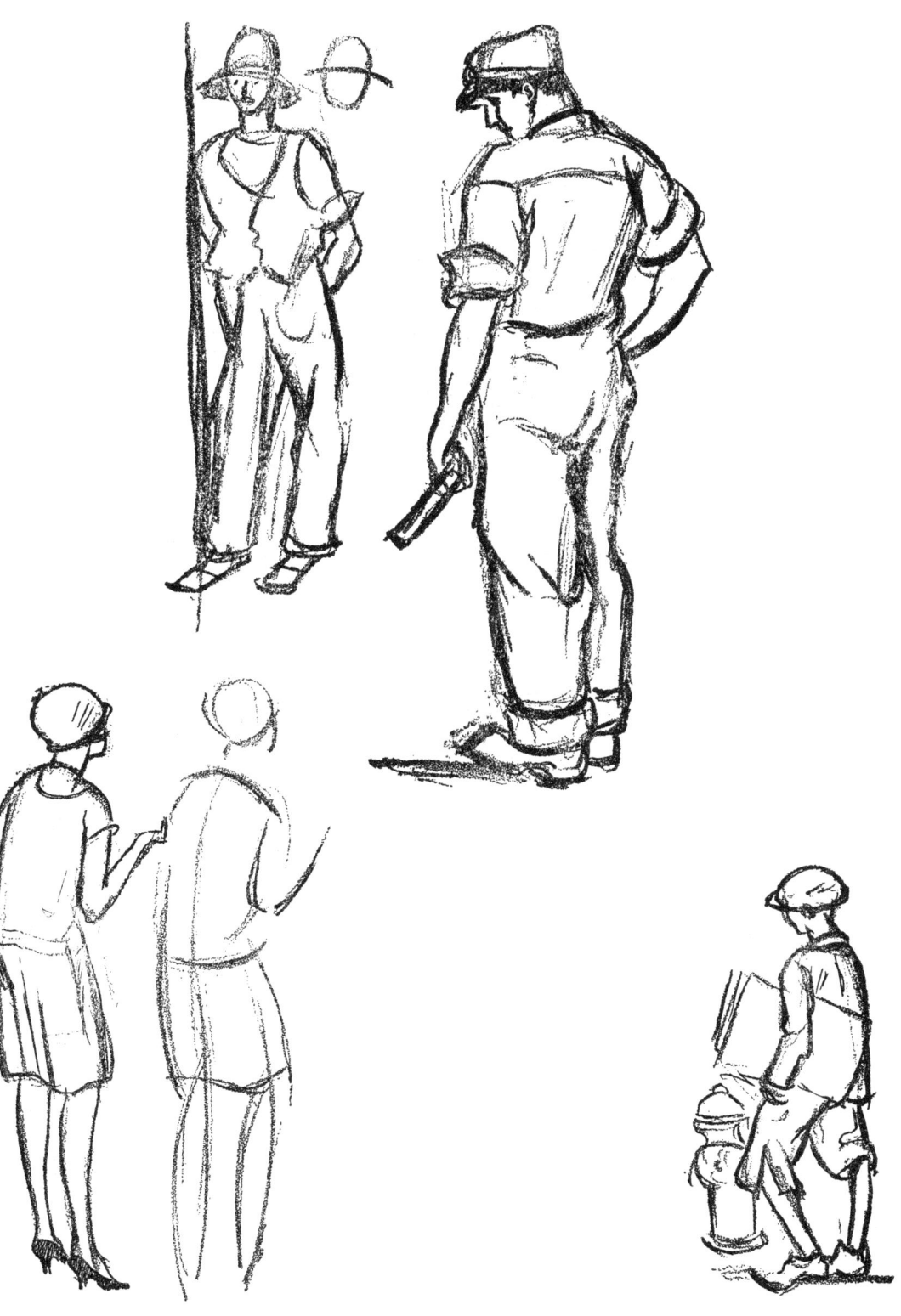

HEADS

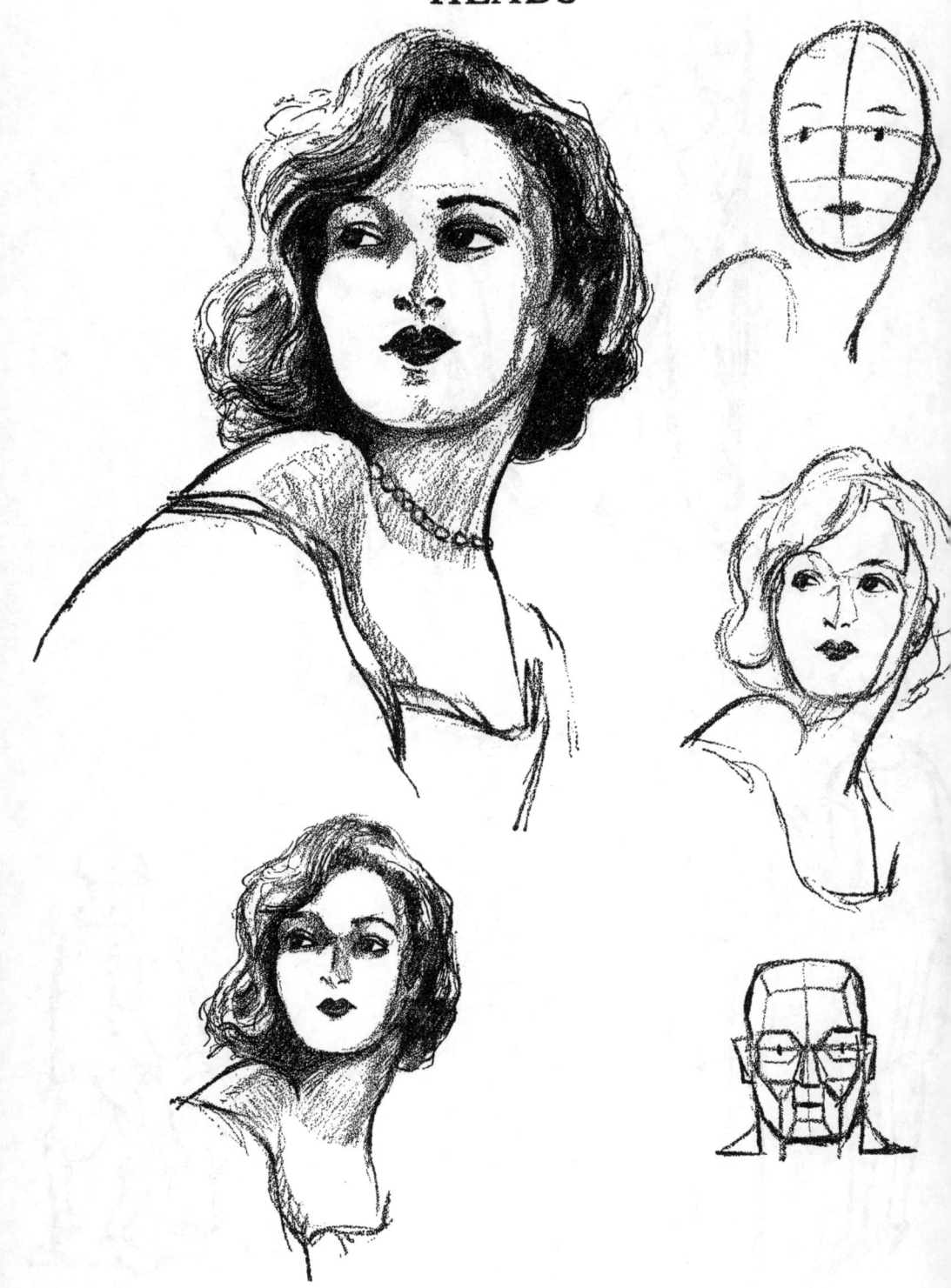

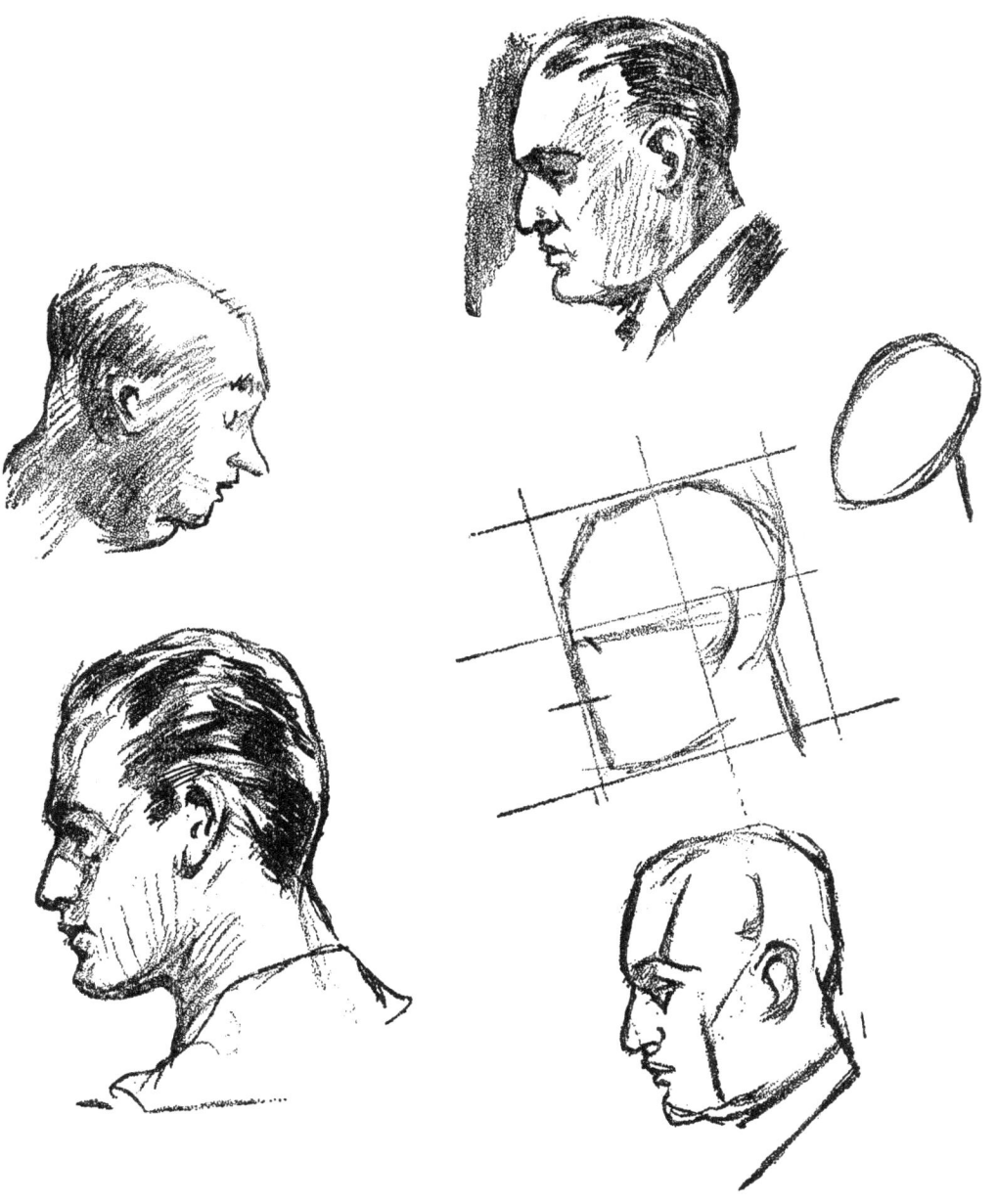

HOW A STORY IS ILLUSTRATED

We will take a story or a part from a story and illustrate it for a line cut reproduction. We will go about this in exactly the same way as it is done for a magazine, taking into consideration the story, type of magazine, decoration of the page, etc.

The Editor gives a layout for the page, showing how much space will be taken up by the title and other descriptive matter pertaining to the story. We are supposed to decorate the rest of the page with a suitable illustration.

We are told that the page is to be kept as light as possible. Light type is being used and the spacing between the lines will be rather wide. The drawing must harmonize with the page, yet enough shade must be used to make the illustration forceful.

The story is laid in the great Northwest. Time about 1890. It deals with an insane preacher and a Killer. A terrific blizzard rages and the Killer, a fugitive from the law, stumbles into the isolated cabin of the preacher. The preacher has queer decorations in his home. Religious texts are painted on the walls and ceiling. In all of them he has the word "Jesus" and the letter "S" is always turned backward. The preacher, aware of the identity of the Killer, tries to force him to give himself up. An argument ensues. Finally, the killer shoots at the persuading one but the bullets seem to have no effect. The preacher stands and points an accusing finger.

The illustration is to be taken from the last of the story, wherein the killer becomes terror-stricken.

A mental picture of that scene forms in the mind.

With this sketch as a base for the design carry it on, and if you find that too many straight lines seem to be running out of the bottom of the picture use another straight line to oppose them, suggesting a table or some article of furniture.

This immediately gives depth to the composition but this new line, however, seems too swift, too unbroken, so add two more shapes to the line opposing it, to suggest other articles of furniture.

Next use a light and dark pattern, remembering to keep the composition as light as possible and yet have enough strong contrast to give it force.

Having now a plan of light and dark, a design which pleases, construct another rectangle of the same proportions as the sketch, only larger—a more convenient space in which to complete the picture.

Following the plans of the sketches, place the design in the new rectangle.

Next, make sketches from a model for the figures and refine them as suggested in the previous pages. Make the necessary changes in character and costume from material available. Refine these until they suit you, then copy on the new rectangle only the big shapes.

The various details are now added, working over the entire composition at the same time, never stopping to finish any single thing. Give the costumes, the character of the heads, hands, furniture, decorations, prominence relative to their value in the picture. The picture is to be entirely completed in pencil. Then use ink over the pencil, following it as carefully as possible.

Note the simplicity of the entire composition.

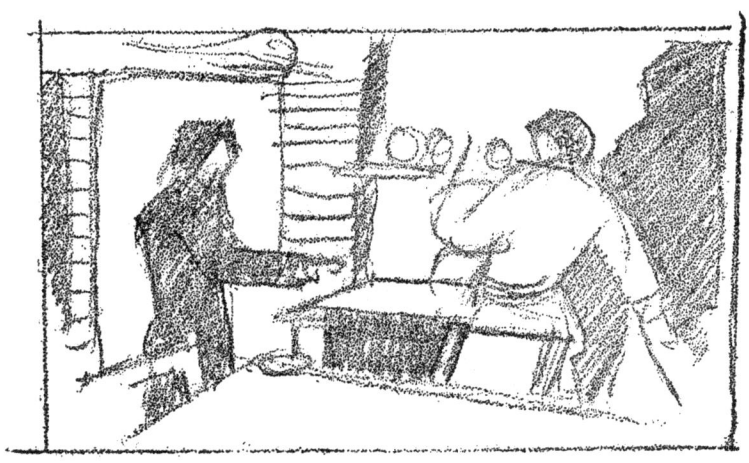

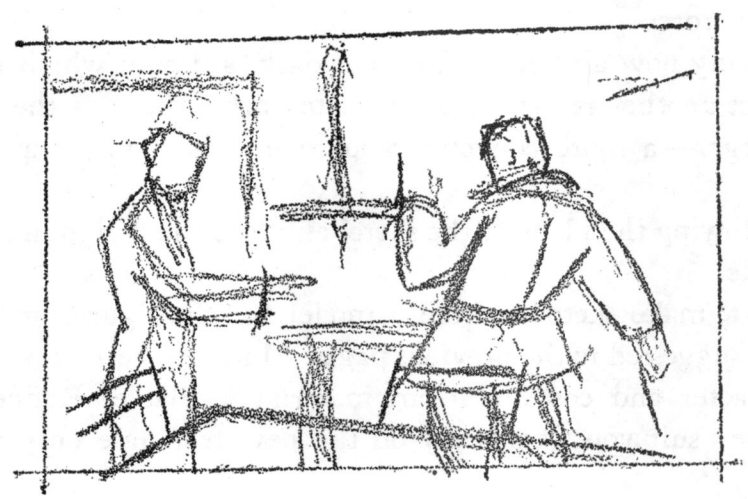

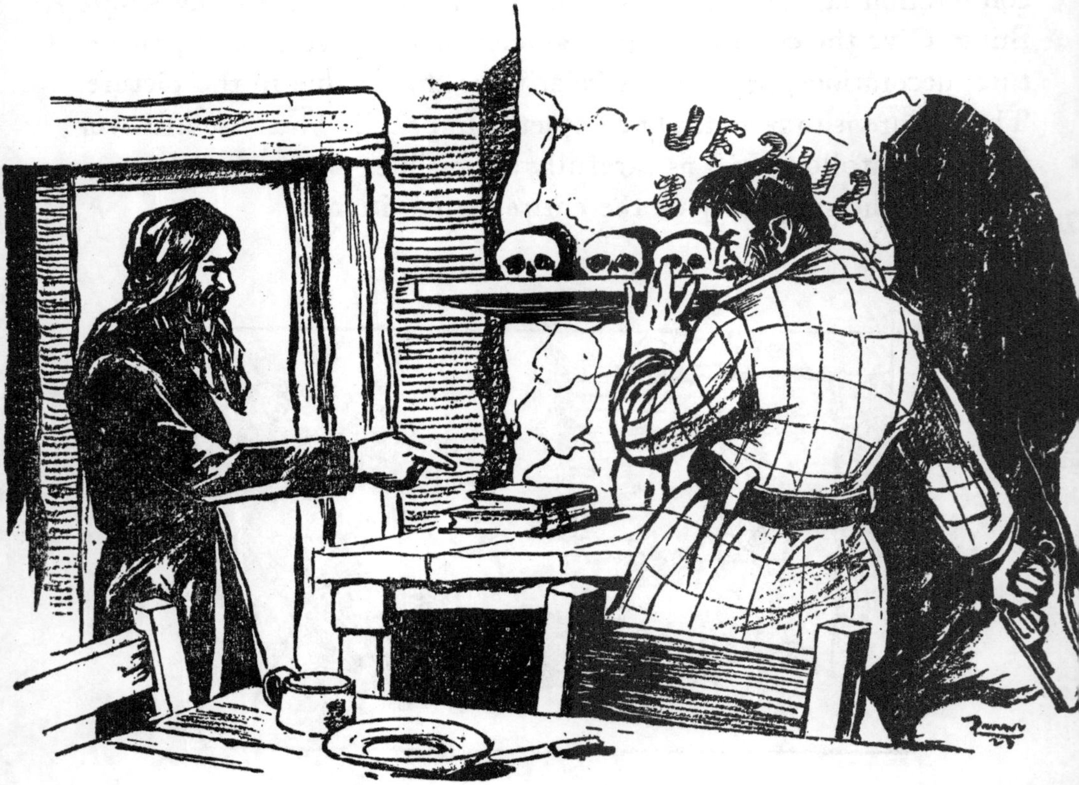